Healer

22 Expert Healers Share Their Wisdom To Help You Transform

Compiled by Kyra Schaefer

Healer: 22 Expert Healers Share Their
Wisdom To Help You Transform

As You Wish Publishing, LLC
Kyra@asyouwishpublishing.com 602-592-1141

ISBN-13: 978-1-7324982-2-8
ISBN-10: 1-7324982-2-9
Library of Congress Control Number: 2019900529

Compiled by Kyra Schaefer
Edited by Todd Schaefer

Printed in the United States of America.

Nothing in this book or any affiliations with this book
is a substitute for medical or psychological help. If you are
needing help please seek it.

Dedication

To all the master teachers in our lives who have taught us
to love and heal.

Table of Contents

Foreword
by Kyra Schaefer

Who are Healers?

Healers are people who have dedicated their lives to learning the truth about themselves. As a result of learning this truth, they take a multitude of self-discovery journeys which direct them toward various methodologies to help them grow.

Once healers have learned about themselves through these journeys, they often want to share their wisdom and express love. Some healers seem born to heal. These people are considered masters from birth and are naturally filled with the love of the divine and will easily express that love without doubt or regard for their safety.

Often, healers have been subjected to every trauma and challenge imaginable. At their core, they believe there is something more to life and they want to expand, regardless of their circumstances.

Many healers in the western world are first introduced to Reiki, a healing modality brought to our awareness by Dr. Usui, a Japanese teacher who found a way to connect with divine energy and utilize that energy through touch or intention. Healers may also come to their healing understandings through massage, oriental medicine, and meditation. Healers are naturally drawn to books or ancient teachings of eastern philosophy on cultivating mind, body and spirit recognition. A new healer who has faced their fears in new ways may also notice they are receiving the information they need, exactly at the moment they need it.

Dispelling Healer Myths

1. Healers are charlatans. They only want to take my money.

On the contrary, most healers are wary of accepting money for their services. A healer may feel that healing work is a gift from God or source and doesn't require payment. I have done more in my line of work as a healer/coach to help healers know their self-worth and accept equal pay for equal energy exchange than anything else I have done. Are there people in the world that may take advantage of you? Yes. However, I feel confident in saying that 98% of the time, a healer genuinely wants to help.

2. Healing work isn't real. What do they think, that I'm going to get touched and get better?

It's real. I have seen miracles happen with my own eyes. I have worked with countless healers to help me through the dark night of my soul. Without the healers in my life, I am certain I would no longer be here. My very first healer was Heather Dunning, an author in this book. She was my first healer, and 20 years later, is still a cherished friend.

3. Healers will "fix" me.

First, you aren't broken. We are all responsible for our experiences. Healers are helpmates and guides. They aren't responsible for your journey. If you rely on healers to do your work for you, when they leave your life, you will be left with nothing. Underdeveloped healers might insist that you depend solely on them for your healing; they may not be willing to let you go. Developed healers will cheer you on as you grow, nurture your progress and let you go when you are ready.

4. Healers are too sensitive.

Through natural or trained ability, healers have an awareness of the subtleties in their environments. They recognize the ebbs and flows of energy—the emotional as well as physical distresses of those around them. Healers are often empaths and can feel the emotions of everyone and everything in their presence. As they develop, they may feel overwhelmed, but quickly learn to overcome those challenges as they cultivate their energy more naturally. When healers learn to navigate energetic shifts, they stand in their power and begin to release people, places and things in their lives that no longer serve them. They choose peace over conflict and still maintain their boundaries with love and dignity. Never mistake their kindness as weakness. As I stated before, many healers have been hurt deeply in their past. More than likely, healers have learned to soften from being toughened-up by their circumstances, not the other way around.

5. I shouldn't have to pay a healer.

You aren't paying a healer for results; you are paying for a healer's time and expertise as you would pay for any doctor or lawyer's time and expertise. The difference is that society puts fewer expectations on established professions. We get well, or we don't; you still pay the bill. A common misconception about healing is that we will be cured of all ailments after one session. It doesn't work that way. Each person has an individual way of processing their life. Each person will heal or change their circumstances at their own pace. That being said, a healer's primary mission is to help people. They want to make the world a better place. We all need a partner, someone who will be honest with us and see the potential inside of us. Healers will see the light in you, that tiny spark waiting to shine.

Fundamentally, we are all light. Healers clear the path and stand with you in the darkness until you can embrace your truest self. This goes far beyond any illness, family or social difficulties. Healing work is a transformation of your being, and will potentially bring you back to who you are—truth, beauty, and love.

In Conclusion

This book is filled with information and exercises from expert healers. They have dedicated their lives to search for understanding and grow from their challenges. They came together to share their wisdom and help you on your journey. You may not resonate with everything written in these pages, but I trust that what does resonate will help you better understand yourself and your experiences. I hope that, as you read this book, something in you shifts and you experience more joy and peace as a result.

Kyra Schaefer is a bestselling author and publisher who has worked in the non-traditional healing field for 15 years. She has helped thousands of people on their self-discovery journeys through Clinical Hypnotherapy. Currently, Kyra owns As You Wish Publishing and makes book publishing accessible for aspiring authors who want to write books that help.

CHAPTER

The Story Between The Lines
by Ana Evans

ANA EVANS

I've heard it said that to understand something, you must stand under its authority, allowing yourself to experience it. Few people understand the concept of a wounded healer like Ana Evans. By a tapestry of 'just the right people at just the right time,' Ana has journeyed from victim to survivor to thriver. Now, her story is one of a healer. Over time, her unique experience has afforded opportunities to serve in a variety of capacities with various organizations that work with victims of trauma. Throughout her journey, one thing has become clear: life is not lived fully unless we are helping others find the path to whole,

sustainable healing. She believes that story is an integral part of that process and continues to share her story with as many as have ears to hear it.
www.givegretness.com,
ana.evans@givegreatness.com

Acknowledgments

Angel Salathe (1972-2018) - Thank you for being my loving, hard-assed, compassionate and beautiful teacher. I miss you every day. I feel you every day in all spaces I take up space in and create space for healing. Namaste, my friend. Dina Gilmore: Thank you for reaching out when you needed me and for remembering me when it came time to write this book.

The Story Between the Lines
by Ana Evans

Hello, dear healer. Thank you for joining me today. Grab your favorite drink and have a seat. I have much to share with you. The last twenty years have been a beautiful winding path of my healing, transmuted into helping others navigate their healing path. My story started before I was born. My family legacy was filled with addiction, mental health struggles and domestic violence. I decided a long time ago that I was going to break the cycles that were eating our family alive from the inside. The problem was that I had no tools to do so. I was prone to finding and cultivating incredibly dysfunctional relationships. This all culminated in an intimate relationship that was emotionally, spiritually and physically abusive. After several attempts, I was able to physically leave the relationship, however, he was not willing to let go of me or the relationship and stalked me for a year and a half. He showed no signs of stopping. I went through the process of having my identity changed. Giving up everything was the beginning of my healing journey. It was also the beginning of my journey as a healer.

My healing journey began with my story. I was invited to speak to a group of nursing students preparing for their emergency room rotations. It was then that I realized that telling my story could help others as it helped me to heal. My role in the story was changing from victim to survivor, mentor and healer. As a healer, I have been a speaker, activist, advocate, facilitator, mentor, coach, energetic-spiritual healer and friend. The story I was telling myself morphed into one of courage, strength and empowerment. I was able to move from fighting to listening, encouraging and teaching. My greatest teachers were the healers that were listening to my story and showing me the markers that would guide me to healing. They did not tell me how, when or what to do. They heard me, asked me questions and offered resources that would help me find my way. In other words, they didn't carry me. They took my hand and walked with me through the painful and healing parts of my journey. They helped me to find the story between its lines that I believed to be true. That changed everything.

So, dear healer, what is your story? Our stories are intertwined in the most intricate ways. My story is changing by writing this. Yours is changing by reading it. We are now a part of each other's stories. This is true for every interaction that you will have with teachers, students and clients, even in your personal relationships. We teach to learn and learn to teach. Let each of your interactions reflect this. Their story, and the way your clients tell it, will tell you where they are in their journey. Your story and how you tell it will tell you where you are in yours. You must pay attention to both. Listen to the stories, look for the beauty, courage, strength and resiliency between the lines.

Journal Prompt:

One of the most effective writing exercises that I've done and shared with clients is a timed writing period. Authors Julia Cameron and Natalie Goldberg use different versions of this writing prompt to break through personal and creative blocks. Either set aside 30 minutes or 3 pages for writing. Use the method that will cause the least distraction for you. Then, write whatever comes to you. If you don't know what to write, write about that. The only rule here is, do not stop writing. Let whatever comes, come. It's going to be messy, feel whiny, and repetitive. Don't be discouraged. Keep going—everyday. Do not go back to read what you have written yet. Give yourself at least a month, then go back and read it all. Get comfortable and settle in. Read it all in one sitting. Have a notebook and pen nearby. Now, look for patterns. This is not an exercise to beat yourself up. There will be successes to record and honor. There will also be pieces of your story that are not in alignment with who you want to be. Write those down and get ready to work on those!

Clients and students will often ask me to sit with them as they read through their first round of writing. This prompt can cause deep anxiety and trigger those who are early in their healing journey. You will know your client. Do what your intuition tells you. My response has varied from sitting with them through the whole process to having them do it on their own and bring in their notes to help them work out the next steps on their journey. Although it can be time-consuming, it is an excellent way to get insight into your client and where they are in their process.

Get to know the healers in your community. They are everywhere. They are in business, criminal justice and the healing arts. They are also people that you meet on the street. If they are holding space for people to be where they are and guiding them towards growth, empowerment and their greatness, then they are healers. Pay attention to and honor the healers around you. Get to know who they are and the different healing modalities that they use. We are all different, and the modalities that work for you may be different than what will work for your clients. Keep this in mind as you begin to create a community of healing partners for your practice.

Journal Prompt:

Let's take a look at the healers who are part of your community. Make a list of the healers around you. Don't forget the teachers, poets, welders and therapists. Whoever is doing healing work in your life should be on the list. Next, determine whether they are a personal or professional connection. Personal connections are the healers in our lives who are not intentionally seeking out clients or students as healers. These are the people who inspire you, who you would like to emulate in your life and practice. Professional connections are those who have active healing practices to whom you would be willing to refer your clients. Write down what it is about your personal connections that inspires you. What about the way they *be* in the world inspires you or makes you want to emulate them? Now, write down the modalities that your professional contacts practice. What does the practice look like? What are the anticipated results? Do they work with a specific population? Is it a one-time practice or one that requires an extended commitment from the client? Initiate relationships with the professional healers with whom you would like to work.

Now, go experience as many of those modalities as you can. This will help you in your healing process and growth. You will learn which modalities are effective in guiding you through your healing. This is a fantastic way to find new modalities to use in your practice. It creates space for you to incorporate those modalities or to refer clients out to someone who may be better equipped to help your client. We have to remember that unless we are talking about our own healing, healing is not about us. We must be careful not to let our egos convince us that we need to be all things to all of our clients. This is dangerous, not only to our well-being and healing, but also to our clients.

It is imperative that we remember we are part of our clients' healing journey. They have invited us into their story. They are looking to us to help them find the mile markers that will guide them in the direction that they want to go. We may walk the entire journey with them. We must also be prepared to be a stepping stone, a momentary connection, to guide them to the healer who can best help them next.

The clients and students who I work with are generally survivors of domestic violence and/or sexual assault. I am often the healer that they believe they need and want. However, there have been clients over the years whose stories have triggered me. Early in my practice, I tried to push through and continue to work with them. I was doing both of us a disservice by letting my ego tell me that I should be able to walk through this with them in a healthy and empowering way. What I have learned to do is step back and recognize when I am not the best healer for the next part of their journey. I will first refer the client to one of my professional connections. Then I reach out to either one of my personal or professional connections to work through the trigger that caused me to pause. Initially, it felt like I was letting both of us down. This was another lie that ego was trying to tell me. The truth? The clients that went to other healers had incredible results. I was able to process and let go of the story that caused the trigger for me. I didn't lose my clients; many of them came back to me for further work. Professional connections to whom I had made referrals began referring clients to me. When I chose to act in integrity for myself and my client, instead of out of fear about how I would look, everyone grew.

Journal Prompt:

Have you had clients who were not a good fit for you or your practice? What was the reason? How did you handle it? Do you feel like it was resolved in a way that was empowering to both you and your client? What strategy worked well for you? What could you have done differently?

I want to acknowledge the clients who don't come back. I blamed myself for a long time. In some cases, there were things I could have done differently, a different choice of words or healing modality. There are times when their story is too much to bear. They thought they were ready and realized that they were not ready. These clients tend to exit my practice in one of two ways. They will either "ghost," and I will not hear from or see them again or they will blame me. The second response can be disheartening for the healer. They will find a way to blame you for their departure. Dear healer, always be willing to look at yourself and your actions to be accountable for any wrongdoing or mistake that may happen. If you are working from a place of integrity and have done what you know to be true and right, release yourself from any drama that may come from this scenario. Release the client with love and prayers for their continued healing.

This is another excellent opportunity to reach out to your connections to talk through the scenario and help hold you accountable in your practice.

Each of us is a work in progress. You will continue to face new challenges and opportunities as you and your practice grow. Your practice will change and become the glorious healing space it is meant to be. We are story-changers, for ourselves and for our clients. The catalyst to healing is often a story filled with fear, pain and suffering. Our work is to find the story between the lines. The story shifts from "I am a victim" to "I survived" to "I choose to live." That is an incredibly powerful transformation. We are birthing healers. They may not start their practice, though some will. They will walk into the world standing taller, empowered and aware of the strength and courage they always carried. People in their circle will be healed because of their healing; the healing of community and the healing community will grow.

Our stories matter. Our voices matter. We can effect change. We don't stand alone. In community, we find our stories and write new ones. In community, we hold each other up when voices and bodies are shaking. In community, we find the strength, courage and love to speak our truth, fight for what is right and shine light into the dark places. Truth heals; light heals. We are healers; we are protectors. As we move out into the world and work, we must take care of each other. Hear each other's stories and honor them. Hold each other up. I am here to hear and honor your stories. The best advice that I can give you is to do your work, learn your story and learn how to tell it. Then honor your clients as they tell you theirs.

CHAPTER

Two

Tangled Web
by Andrea Sommer

ANDREA SOMMER

Andrea Sommer is a best-selling published author, blogger and single mother to three amazing children. She shares her stories and insights with the hope that they assist others in realizing that it is easier to overcome adversity when we realize our strengths and abilities. She is passionate about healthy living and has received training in Reflexology, Touch for Health, Yoga and is a Reiki Master. She invites you to connect with her a
andreasommer@live

Acknowledgments

Pierrette Boutin, Odette Karlsson, Kara-Lynn Palmer, Jackie Kavanagh and Michal Morgan

A Tangled Web
by Andrea Sommer

*A*bandoned. The walls were closing in. Tall. Dark. Foreboding. The room was cold, vacant. Still. So quiet you could hear a pin drop. Here she sat. Cross-legged. Motionless. Head in her hands. Arms folded in her lap. Uncertain. Rigid. Yet, beautiful to an onlooker in her vulnerability. Sensitive. Authentic.

Calm femininity permeated from her, yet she feared it to the point that it caused her to sit alone in this room, frozen in fear. Completely and utterly immobilized. The doors seemed locked to her. How was she to escape this room? How would she be able to stand? Would there be enough strength in her legs to carry her? If there was, what lay beyond the door? Was there help on the other side of this door? Could they help her? If not, then why get up?

Many of us have visited this tangled web of darkness and challenge. So please, don't ever believe you are alone and need to remain in solitude, nor should your pain remain unspoken. Life is not always easy, and many challenges are thrown our way. We sit, we stand, we think, we fall, we feel, we fear, we hurt, and then we scream, "Why the hell are we stuck here? Why am I in this? Why me?" The unfortunate reality to living this human experience is this: it's all part of life. This has pissed me off every time I've heard it, and it still upsets me when I'm facing a challenge. We are all souls living the human experience. However upsetting and frustrating, this is the darkness where the most growth occurs. We go through losses, hurts, physical, mental and psychological pain. However, all too often, we continue to seek out others to heal us. Only *we* truly know how *we* feel— where we feel it and how it hurts. We need to acknowledge that *we are our best healer*. We can all be experts in our own right. I understand it's difficult to feel empowered and guided when all you see around you is fog.

When healing one's self, it's important to bring together many modalities to bring your body back to a gentle state of homeostasis. Homeostasis is defined as "a healthy state that is maintained by the constant adjustment of biochemical and physiological pathways." Having a clean, healthy diet is imperative for healing. The reason I say this is because, in many ancient cultures, such as in healing lodges, healing was practiced with simplicity. It's imperative to have an opportunity to reflect within. Unfortunately, in our society today, at the pace that we rotate our tires and we participate in daily life, we're no longer offering our bodies an opportunity to remain quiet. We become entangled in a web of toxins: chemicals, emotions and circumstances. They are not necessarily toxic in the pure definition of toxicity but, rather, toxic to who we innately are.

As defined by modern quantum physics in 1925, everything is energy! We are all linked to one another on this earth like chess pieces playing a game. We share similar anatomy, similar fears, similar ailments, and hence, similar challenges. Whether we sit across from our family doctor to share a host of symptoms, visit our psychotherapist and share our fears and resulting sleepless nights, or sit with our Reiki practitioner who uses energy to assist us in bringing our bodies back into balance, we are all energy. So here you see.

There is nothing to fear in being authentic and allowing one to exchange energy for assisting us in our healing. It's better than remaining cold and frozen in fear. This is beauty!

We each possess the ability to not only listen for words or sounds, but also to abide by our fear instincts. When we look inward and trust our intuition, we allow it to guide us to the steps necessary in our healing journey. If we are feeling "off," intuition can let us know that perhaps it is time to go to the doctor. When I was a child, I loved the "choose your own adventure" books. As I get older, I see that these books were brilliant! Life is a "choose your own adventure" book. As we stop on page 6, we have this big, monster Sasquatch standing in front of us and our body is *riddled* with fear.

Here we have an opportunity to either fast forward to page 65 or go to page 240, both ultimately contributing to a different scene depending upon which page we choose! If we were to look at our own healing in this context, why not follow our curiosity as we did at the age of eight? Feel and identify the fear and allow yourself to become vulnerable. In doing so, ask a question to your body: "Where do I go from here?" We're all part of a larger community like chess pieces walking on this beautiful earth. For the most part, we carry similar anatomy. Yet, we are fearful of accessing and demonstrating our vulnerability and allowing ourselves to share our fears. Ultimately, doing so will open up doors rather than close them. It allows us to become more accessible and permits those who are willing to be able to assist us. In the book, *The Gift of Fear*, Gavin de Becker helps us to understand this gut feeling. Intuition or fear can assist us tremendously in keeping us safe and listening to ourselves. It will send a definite signal in a moment when we need to remove ourselves from a situation which is harmful to us. This same signal can also arrive if something in our body isn't right.

Chronic busyness decreases your ability to love yourself. Don't allow yourself to be consumed by inadequacy. Don't give up your power! The greatest healing comes from taking back your power. In doing so, you empower yourself to grow. The beauty is that you are never alone on the journey. Others are always on this journey with you, as you are never solitary in existence. Thankfully, there are healers whom you will meet along your journey to assist you in navigating the tide back to shore.

By going through these difficult initiations, we are prepared for leadership roles. Let the leadership begin with you!

These eight easy steps will assist you in accessing your valuable intuition and ultimately guide you on your healing journey.

1. Identify and release your core beliefs.

We all carry around core beliefs about ourselves. They are formed from the time we are born and continue to be shaped by events in our lives, our environments growing up and our interactions with others. These beliefs place us on autopilot which is firm on its course and, therefore, will challenge us with anything that is deemed risky by being new or outside of our respective comfort zones.

In this process, it's important to identify and be truthful about what we think about ourselves while feeling the negativity and holding onto the pain in our hands and accept everything that has happened to us along the way. Only then do we allow ourselves the opportunity to move forward and trust our intuition. In my experience, much of this can be tied to our inner child. An example of this might be when you were ten years old and weren't picked to be a part of the class baseball team. It can be as simple as that, and have a surprisingly cumulative effect.

2. Let go of victimhood thinking.

Most of us have matured in a world that was far from the perfect life. Often times, we hold onto the great memories and hide away the not so great ones. Our inner child remembers as an 8-year-old being slapped and asked to stay in our room. This resulted in us embedding negative emotions when not being heard. We need to hold onto this pain and allow ourselves to work through it with the comprehension of an adult while embracing the 8-year-old child.

3. Listen to your gut instinct.

All too often, we intellectualize and disregard those nagging feelings. Or, we proceed solely on the advice of another. As we listen to our gut instincts, it becomes easier to distinguish the feeling of a true fear versus something meant for our highest good by presenting itself outside of our comfort zone. The answer is always within us when we listen to our gut instincts and follow the heart's voice. These sensations are there for a reason.

4. Uncover meditation.

Many speak about the importance of meditation. I prefer to call this "remaining in stillness." After 20 years of trying,

I am *still* not great at sitting for an hour on my meditation pillow. I suggest sitting cross-legged on a meditation pillow or bench. This can be uncomfortable for many when starting out, and quite discouraging. I associate meditation to the daydreaming we did as children. Be gentle with yourself and find a position that is comfortable for you. Start with 10 or 15 minutes of sitting in complete stillness. Or perhaps try "walking meditations." I find with my passion for being outside that walking alone outdoors is quite soothing and allows me to quiet my mind. I like being slowly whisked away by the sounds of running water or birds singing. Shamans, especially among certain tribal cultures, are seen as connections between nature (animals, water, trees, plant life and the earth) and humans. Experiment and have fun. You may find that you're most able to connect to self when surrounded by the natural world. Rest, reflect and rejuvenate the mind and body. It provides a healing space to converse with self and assist in pointing you in the next direction. Once the process becomes a practice then, like any skill, you get better at it and it serves to sharpen your intuition.

5. Forgive self-harm.

We each have our own forms of self-harm: over-indulging, isolating, consuming excess alcohol or self-medicating. But the biggest harm we do to ourselves is staying stuck and ignorant in our beliefs that we aren't worthy or that we are okay to remain in emotional or physical pain. Stuck is not okay! Our bodies want to assist us in any opportunity to heal to the best of our ability. When we step away from self-harm—when we begin to look at ourselves with compassion and forgiveness—we begin to let down the guard that wants to punish us and, instead, fill up that space with loving mindfulness. We can begin to tap into our gut on a deeper level.

6. Break the bonds of attachments and resentments.

Purge. In my younger years, I liked to accumulate old books, clothing items I hadn't worn in years, the junk drawer, a pile of unworn jewelry, and most importantly, anger and resentments I'd let fester and grow. I was hanging onto the *feelings* that were attached to these things. But these feelings weren't light, and this weighed down my energy and belief in myself. In allowing ourselves to release our stranglehold on deep-rooted resentments and attachments, we are giving ourselves permission to let go fully. In doing so, we create a space in which we can relax with renewed belief in ourselves, assisting us in listening to and relying on our intuition. Feng shui is an excellent way to gently assist you in purging the clutter and allowing you to only hold onto what speaks to your heart.

7. Embrace yourself.

In our human condition, it's easy to get into the habit of compulsively searching, rushing from one thing to the next and keeping ourselves distracted from nagging, uncomfortable feelings. In my experience, it was important to go from one healer to the next, hoping someone would help. As this road of healing becomes ever more familiar, it's easy to stay committed. It's even possible to become addicted to healing. But do yourself a favor and choose your next adventure. Open the next page and stop running away from yourself and, instead, *run toward yourself.* Embrace yourself and know that you have the answers. When we are at ease in our vessels, we begin to feel secure in the world and we are able to branch out while listening to our intuition.

8. Self-Discipline.

It's important to set small, achievable goals and write them down or put them on your cell phone's calendar. Otherwise, in the whirlwind of healing ourselves, it can become overwhelming. What are some goals for the day, the week, the month or the year? It is helpful to set an intention and formulate a plan or direction. The simpler, the better, especially when starting out. Do you want to journal daily, meditate, start a yoga practice or stop consuming sugar? Write it down. When will it take effect? When will you check in to evaluate your progress? Who will you consult for ideas? Which pieces of literature would assist you to locate information of interest or find referrals to healers?

We are all a work in progress. It takes patience, discipline and a desire for self-discovery. Have fun in your healing journey. What you will uncover about yourself will be amazing. Focus on both your mind *and* your body, not just one or the other. We are created as one vessel and everything works in perfect synchronicity. Embrace your inner child and open the book to choose your adventure. Follow your developing intuition to what sparks your curiosity. I have found that this is the body's way of awakening us to what may not only be super cool, but may also be what lights up the darkness on the next inner discovery. Once your intuition speaks to you and you begin to have a clearer understanding of what it is trying to show you, profound healing can occur and inner strength can develop. It is of utmost importance that you remember that you are *listening to* and not *discarding* your inner voice and, ultimately, that is doing the greatest honor for yourself.

CHAPTER

Three

Inner Beauty Transformation
by Audrey Rai

AUDREY RAI

Audrey Rai is a certified psychic medium, yoga instructor, energy healer and spiritual mentor who has devoted her life to working with *spirit*. She empowers others in person and remotely by creating a safe learning platform for exploring their spiritual gifts, receive healing and providing a supportive community in a non-competitive platform. Connecting with *spirit*, guides, angels and ancestors, Audrey taps into the collective consciousness for messages and healing to support you on your unique journey. Audrey specializes in mentoring women, children and men who value their sacredness. She illuminates the inner wisdom of lightworkers, empowering them to open to their gifts and soul contracts. Audrey is heart-centered as she allows herself to be the conduit for you to receive a clear and open channel of messages and healing for the highest good of all. www.audreyrai.com audreyraimedium@gmail.com

Acknowledgments:

Thank you to my family for trusting the visionary in me along this journey. Thank you to Sarah Amala for your wisdom, love, support and help with my writing. Thank you to Sharon Muzio & Kellie Munns for guiding me to this path that supports the healing work and teaching that I came into this world to do. Thank you to my Lily Dale sisters for encouraging and validating me. Last, but not least, thank you to my beautiful community at Blackberry & Maple for bringing your love and light into the world and trusting me to guide you on your unique journeys. Your support waters the seeds of my soul. You are all my teachers and bring unmeasurable joy into my life. I love you and have tremendous gratitude for all of you.

Inner Beauty Transformation
by Audrey Rai

In 2010, I was disconnected from my soul. was the owner of a busy salon in Central Pennsylvania, I worked twelve hour days without breaks and made myself available at all times to my staff and clientele. Between my job, raising two children and keeping a marriage afloat, I had no time even to consider tapping into myself, nor was I aware of the concept. My body, however, decided it was time for a change. Plantar fasciitis, loss of sleep, and lower back pain benched me from my usual rigorous schedule—which threw me into a panic. All I could think about was how I would sustain my income. How would I fix my body so that it could keep up with my life?

I decided that surgery as the best option and began looking into disability insurance. At the same time, a client recommended that I look into acupuncture. For reasons beyond me, I decided to follow up on that recommendation. I found myself sitting in a room with my new acupuncturist, explaining that I had no time to eat my meals and held my bladder for twelve hours at a time. "Your body is trying to talk to you," he told me. "You are not a machine." I didn't agree with him at first. To me, my body was a machine. But as we began our treatments, something began to shift in me. During one session, I began to see lava-like blobs of colorful light. When I asked him what they were, he simply said, "You saw your energy." "Okay," I thought to myself. "Sure."

At this same time, I began practicing yoga. I needed a low-impact workout while my body was healing, and I was impressed by the figures of the women on the cover of *Yoga Journal*. It was quickly made clear to me that yoga would be much more than a workout in my life. I learned how to take a full breath. I learned how to pull my attention inward. Those colorful blobs I had seen during acupuncture became much more common and I began to hear things. My intuition was waking up and the call to change my life was deep and all-encompassing.

Over the next year, I gobbled up every metaphysical book I could get my hands on and attended dozens of workshops on spirituality. I studied different forms of energy work, and parts of myself that I had suppressed began bubbling to the surface. I began to remember myself and allow myself to believe in the angelic beings that have consistently come to me throughout my life. They have always been with me, and despite what adults had told me, they were real. I recalled an incident at church camp from when I was thirteen. I had a deck of tarot cards in my suitcase, and because of that, I was sent home and shamed for not being in alignment with God. Armed with that confidence and opening to energy, I began to connect with my spirit guides. They shared with me that, when I was a child, I shut down my magic because I was afraid. Of course I was—no adult believed me and no adults in my life knew how to nurture my gifts.

Remembering this led me down the path of working with children to normalize similar experiences for them. As I work with children, my inner child is delighted and also begins to heal. As I continue down this path, it's not all sparkles and fairy dust. I feel so much shame, fear, heartache and disappointment as the friendships that had been my "center" up until that point began to disintegrate. I even feel a disconnection with my family and the guilt is so strong. After all, they didn't ask for any of this. They didn't want me to change, and the changes I am driven to make are often different from their expectations. Eventually, I came to learn that these judgments have little to do with me and a lot to do with other people's insecurities, fears and low vibrations.

As old friendships fall away, however, others on a similar path begin to show up. This lifts my heart and gives me the confidence I need to finally sell my salon and use that money to open a healing space on my property where I offer energy work, crystal healing, yoga, workshops and coach others.

Slow and gentle are my new ways of living. I learn to create boundaries with others, with love for myself and for them. As I settle into this new rhythm of being, my gifts begin to deepen. Energy begins to flow through my hands during meditation. At times, my arm involuntarily lifts. My hand then makes these repetitive movements. I come to learn that these are called "mudras," and are an ancient way of connecting with spirit and enhancing meditation. Spirit guides me where to place my hands on the body, what mudras to make and how to work with crystals and herbs for healing. During this time, I was seeking community and guidance outside of myself. Spirit gave me a strong message to stop seeking human teachers and to start learning directly through my connection to spirit. "No more classes," I heard. I listened.

One day, my intuition was taken to a whole new level. Spontaneously, *spirit* started talking to me and giving me long messages for people. Not only was I given visions for them about their future and path, but I also connected with their loved ones in spirit. Up until this point, I might have worked on a client, smelled tobacco and intuitively knew that their grandfather was hanging around, but this was different. I felt a deeper connection to spirit and could now have entire conversations with people who had left their physical bodies whom I have never met. Friends brought their friends, who were strangers to me. I gave them mediumship readings from their loved ones, angels and spirit guides. At times, I was guided to lay hands on them for channeled healing. I scanned their bodies and shared with accuracy what ailments they and their deceased loved ones had. Often, spirit tells me a list of foods they should be eating to improve their health. Sometimes, a whole business plan comes through, shedding light on their life's purpose.

It is evident that healing (not to be confused with healed) is occurring from these messages I channel. Not only energetic healing, but also emotional healing. These messages reduce the fear of death. Grief around a loved one passing shifts into a different perspective with this new awareness. Recently, I read for a longtime salon client/friend who lost her daughter in a horrific accident 25 years ago. The daughter gave me beautiful messages to share with her mother. She showed me what she looked like the last time she saw her, what she was wearing, the style of her hair and things they talked about. What spirit did not tell me was that this woman would have a stroke and leave her physical body two weeks later. I was sad to lose my friend in her physical form, but quickly connected to her in spirit. I am a little sad but happy that she is reconnected with her daughter.

So what am I? A psychic? A medium? An intuitive? A healer? A yoga instructor? A spiritual mentor? Whereas before in my life, I could label myself clearly, it now feels so limiting because I am all of these things and so much more and hear that there is more to come. These gifts are seamlessly blended together. When you have a reading with me, whether it is in person or remotely, you are also receiving energy work. When you are receiving energy healing with me, you are also receiving messages from your loved ones in spirit, spirit guides and angels. It is all healing, whether it is hands-on, channeled messages or medicine from the Earth such as crystals and herbs. The more we seek guidance from teachers outside of our inner wisdom, the more we are labeled and put into a box. Our gifts and healing styles are unique and should be celebrated. Finding a tribe that promotes your growth is essential. It is simple: the more that you share in the successes of your tribe, the more the tribe collectively grows and the more you grow. Find those people who support you. Create strong boundaries with those that don't.

In doing this work, healthy boundaries with everyone in your life are essential to your spiritual growth. Some of the people in your life are going to have a hard time when you implement your new boundaries. I had to learn to say no and prioritize my wants and needs to create the space to connect with spirit. Spiritual work takes a lot of self-care. Whatever you think you need, multiply it at least by two. Not everyone in my life understands that. To be of service to *spirit*, I put spirit guidance before all others and trust that the rest will be taken care of.

This is the journey that I am now on and I wouldn't trade it for status, money or beauty. I am honored to share my gifts with anyone looking for comfort or guidance on their path. My life is about having experiences and spreading love and comfort in every way that I can. I lead from my heart and deliver messages and healing from God, angels and loved ones in spirit. How incredible is that? There are no amount of words that can express my gratitude towards God for my gifts, but I still try every day and ask Him to allow me opportunities to be of service to Him.

Your higher self knows everything. There are two important keys to growing as a healer and lightworker: trust and surrender. When you feel disconnected and out of alignment with trust and surrender, consider asking your higher self, spirit guides, angels and ancestors for guidance. Recognize that the thoughts in your head and the messages that you receive are all coming to you in the same voice— yours. This is why most people miss their intuitive "hits" and dismiss them and their thoughts and as coincidences. It is important to learn to distinguish the difference between what is your thought and what is a message. The breath is where you can deepen your connection. If, at any time, you feel as though you are losing your connection while doing healing work or channeling messages, bring yourself back to your breath, ground your energy down and ask for a clearer connection. Following is an exercise that you can record and listen to or go to my webpage where I have recorded it for you. I suggest that you use this exercise regularly and I encourage you to share it with workshops that you lead.

Find a comfortable position sitting or lying down. Ground your energy down by connecting with your breath and taking your attention inward. Close your eyes and roll them up and inward toward your third eye space. This is your sixth chakra, Ajna. By doing this, you are activating your pineal gland and your intuition. Remember, your higher self knows everything and you are able to access anything that you need to know for your highest and best good. Slow down and lengthen your inhale through your nose, and match your exhale back out through your nose.

Continue to focus on your breath. See the air that you are drawing into your body as the healing energy and life force that it is. Envision the air as a soft, velvety ribbon of white or golden light. With each breath, this healing light fills your whole body. Scan your body and notice how you feel. Notice any sensations in the body. If you discover any stuck energy or anything else that no longer serves you, draw your next breath in through your nose to this stagnant energy, then send it down through your spine and into the Earth where it can be repurposed into something more useful.

The Earth is always there for you, nurturing you, nourishing you and holding you. Begin to notice and observe your thoughts. Notice that there is a difference between your words and the messages that are being intuited to you. Ask your guides to help you distinguish the difference between the two. Continue to connect with your breath and observe what you notice as you become aware of the difference between the ego and your intuition. Do not judge yourself. Allow and continue to observe what comes in as you stay connected with your breath. Your breath is your connection to spirit and your intuition.

Ask your higher self the following:

- What do I need to know at this time?
- Are there any messages to assist me on my journey?
- What can I do to support my healing?

Ask your higher self to step to the forefront of your awareness and guide you throughout your day. Thank your higher self for always being there for you. Notice how you feel. Start to come back to your awareness and back into your body. Begin to make small movements with your fingers and toes. Take a moment to feel gratitude for yourself and all that it took for you to carve this time out of your day for your healing. Namaste.

CHAPTER

Four

Gifts From The Soul
by Christine Salter

CHRISTINE SALTER

Christine Salter is a psychic and evidentiary medium, spiritual teacher, and healer who is passionate about assisting grieving people in opening their spiritual gifts of spirit communication. She is a contributing author in *Happy Thoughts Playbook* and has presented for national conferences targeting grief. Christine is dedicated to supporting people on their spiritual and healing journeys so that they may reclaim their inner light that was dimmed by the passing of a loved one.

Acknowledgments

I want to thank all of the incredible bereaved parents that I have had the pleasure to work with. Your strength and resilience to overcome your fears and connect with your kids is always amazing to see. The bond between parent and child is eternal. To the kids in spirit, thank you for helping your parents and giving them the gift of your love. You are the best cheerleaders for your parents' growth! I give special thanks to my team for helping me help others: Nikki Elliot, Cathy Lind, Stephanie Larmore, Alma Redding-Kyle, and Amy Campbell. Love you all!

Gifts from the Soul
by Christine Salter

The loss of a loved one can be a catastrophic experience for many people. In an instant, their lives are changed forever. The familiarity of daily routines has shattered into a million pieces, and nothing makes any sense. With so much uncharted territory in front of them, they might receive help to finish the unfinished business of someone's earthly existence. Friends and loved ones may momentarily rush in, bringing love and comfort while everything feels like a blur. They are grateful for the distraction of having company while they barely survive the fog of a new reality that they don't recognize. Grief is overwhelming, like an ocean coming in waves, knocking them under, emotionally. Once the dust settles, everyone goes back to their lives as if nothing has happened. Still in shock and disbelief, they sit with the shards of what is now their life, wondering how this can be. It doesn't matter if this loss was expected or sudden, the shattering is the same.

As the days wear on, they are left staring at the pieces on the floor, wondering if they will ever put them back together. Some large shards have survived and other parts have been crushed to dust. Their life doesn't make any sense as they feel wave after wave of grief wash over them. They may feel like they are drowning and can't catch their breath, longing for their old life back and for this pain to go away. Feeling alone, they wonder if anyone cares because all they experience is pain. They have a strong need to talk about their loved one, but it makes others uncomfortable, and they pull away. Like a crazy kaleidoscope, their new existence comes into focus.

These are the experiences that I hear over and over from parents who have lost a child, regardless of how that child passed. The unimaginable has happened, and they are thrust into a giant pit of darkness, full of clawed monsters. This grief-monster digs itself into their flesh and refuses to let go. It is hard to breathe, and they momentarily escape by sleeping or medicating themselves. Life seems to be a series of extremes with no end in sight. Tears are continually flowing, or they freeze and bury their emotions deep within themselves, pretending it hasn't happened and their child is just "away."

Something changes in a parent when their child dies. Their entire belief system is challenged as they are rocked to their core. Some people hold onto their faith and lean on God for their comfort. Others might research the afterlife in an attempt to understand where their child has gone. The desire to know that their child is at peace is a strong motivator, and it can become their primary focus.

Some parents are lucky that their child will give them a sign right after their transition to let them know that they are okay. These parents might already be on a spiritual path, and it is easy for their child to get through. Other parents struggle to find anything, which creates more despair. They have an intense need to receive validation that their child is safe and they might go to great lengths to find out. Finding their child becomes a mission, which leads to their awakening.

One of the gifts of the shattering is that as you search and evolve and you find new truths that may not have resonated with you before. You slowly see the lessons that are presented for your growth even though, at the time, it didn't feel like much good could come from it. As you start to heal and some of the heaviness you experienced starts to lift.

For many, the experience of child loss leads to an intense journey of self-discovery. Your life purpose and the reason that you are on the earth is to evolve your soul. There are many experiences for your soul to choose from in deciding how it is going to grow. The significant people and events in your life are carefully chosen long before your incarnation. From the soul's perspective, this is an opportunity for immense spiritual growth, and things are carefully planned out before you arrive in your human form. The awakening leads you on a spiritual journey that your human self didn't sign up for, but your soul eagerly did.

Once you are born and settled into earth school, your soul starts to work the plan. You may have signed up to experience the duality of specific lessons such as comp-assion, unconditional love, adversity, or acceptance. You may develop your perseverance, gratitude, empathy, or courage. You may sit with doubt, guilt, anger, or fear and need to learn how to work through them. Many people experience grief as a significant component of their lives because it encompasses many lessons all at once.

Your loved ones in spirit are aware of what your soul is learning, and they are cheering you on every step of the way. They know everything that is going on with you and how you feel. There are no secrets in the spirit world. They hear every word you say to them and experience all of the love you have for them. Parents will ask me if their child knows that they are loved and the answer is always the same: they feel the love from your soul to theirs for eternity.

In working with parents, I have found that a variety of emotions can get in the way of having a full connection with their child. Guilt is one of the primary feelings that can block them. Shame and regret also add to the emotional toll that a grieving parent experiences. Guilt comes from the ego or lower self which is the critical voice we hear in our minds. Guilt means that you feel as though you should have done something different. It is heavy, like a massive wet blanket, suffocating all the joy that might try to enter your life. It pretends to be instructive and helpful. Guilt is that voice that says "I should have done more" or "I have failed my child." Guilt is the voice that says "I am your parent and I should have known." It doesn't care that things are far outside of your control and that you did all that you humanely could have. It is always whispering that you didn't do enough. Ultimately, it is a variety of fears designed to keep you stuck and in pain. Being brave and acknowledging guilt can be a painful process.

You need to have the courage to voice the words that you are afraid to voice even if fear says they might be true. Thoughts such as "I failed you" or "I could have done more" only create more fear in an already traumatized person. You might even carry the belief that voicing these fears somehow might make them come true, so you hold them deep inside continuing the cycle. As you start to express these fears and look objectively, you realize that guilt is a mouse, not the lion that it pretends to be. The quickest way to release the energy and pain of guilt, and help bring peace and joy back to your life, is through forgiveness.

Forgiveness is often a misunderstood concept. People tend to erroneously believe that it is about accepting that someone has done something wrong and you are in agreement with their actions. In reality, it is the acceptance that things are as they are and you are releasing the need to hold onto the emotions of the situation. People who choose not to forgive are slowly poisoning their souls. They become hardened, and they slowly wither away, leaving no room for happiness. Bitterness and anger become the dominant feelings, draining away years of their lives.

Forgiveness is the salve that can help heal the wound, created by the passing of a loved one. Self-forgiveness is a powerful medicine that releases the judgment you are carrying about choices you or others made. The truth is that your loved ones want you to be happy and fulfilled in life. There is a mistaken belief that the deeper the pain someone experiences from the passing of a loved one, that it is the measure of how much you love them. Giving up this pain seems to equate to not loving them any longer. The opposite is actually true. Choosing to heal and honor your path helps both of you. Your loved ones see the pain that you sit in. Imagine them asking you, "If the roles were reversed, would you want *me* to be in pain?" They know how much they are loved. They want you to release the pain that you carry so they can reach you in meaningful new ways.

Shoulda, Coulda, Woulda: A Guilt Inventory

Take out two pieces of paper and a pen. Give yourself about 30 minutes of quiet time where you will not be disturbed. Open your heart and be willing to feel and heal.

1. Allow yourself to go into a quiet space mentally and be willing to let your ego speak, even if you are afraid of what it might say.
2. Take the first sheet of paper and write out all of the things that you are guilty for, without holding back. Start each sentence with these words "I should have…"
3. Allow the emotions and energy to flow through the pen. Write until no more thoughts are coming to mind.
4. Next, take your second sheet of paper and lay it down next to your first.
5. On the second paper, replace "I should have" with the following words: "I am willing to forgive myself for not." and then finish writing out your statement.
6. Now, read each statement to yourself, pausing to breathe between each one. Repeat the sentences that feel difficult to accept, opening your heart to the healing that is taking place.
7. When you are finished with your writing session, throw away or burn the papers. This completes the healing by releasing the papers to the universe via trash or fire.
8. You may find that you need to do this exercise regularly. The further you get down the healing

path, the more you may experience unconscious feelings surfacing.

Please read through the instructions before you work with this visualization. You will be using your imagination for this exercise. You may feel like you are making answers up and that is okay. The first things that come to mind are correct. It is important not to overthink what comes to mind. You may also record the following instructions so you can listen to the visualization.

The Balloon Release

1. Imagine that you have a large ball, full of your guilt, on the ground in front of you.
2. How big is the ball and what is its color?
3. Is it light or heavy?
4. Could you easily pick it up?
5. Is it solid or hollow?
6. If you could touch the surface, what does the texture feel like?
7. Notice if there is a string attached to you from this ball.
8. Once you are able to visualize or feel this ball, we will make changes to it using the power of your imagination.
9. In your mind, change the color of the ball to whichever color feels right to you.
10. Next, shrink the ball to the size of a balloon.
11. Imagine that the ball has become hollow, if it wasn't already.

12. Imagine severing any connection that you might have between you and the ball; imagining a pair of scissors or a knife works well for this.
13. Imagine this guilt ball fills with helium and becomes light and bouncy.
14. Toss it up into the air and watch the wind take it away, up into the clouds. Give thanks to spirit for taking the guilt that you freely released.
15. Visualize breathing in white light and fill yourself up with it, allowing it to fill up the spaces where the guilt used to reside.

Choosing to release guilt is a powerful step in reclaiming and rebuilding your life. Every step you take on your healing journey is valuable to your soul, and the lighter you can become, the easier it is to connect with your loved one. Walking a healing path after losing a loved one is full of twists and turns. It is never the straight line that we think it should be. The journey seems to be a spiral that keeps walking us back to experiences that we thought we had mastered, only to discover another facet of the same lesson appears. This is a part of the soul's journey in earth school. Please know that you can't fail at healing. It is a lifelong experience with many starts and stops along the way.

Healing is a choice that only you can make. Many people choose to believe that grief doesn't heal. I work with parents every day that are walking the path to healing and choosing to see the sunshine within the storm. They are getting clear communication from their kids, and they know beyond a shadow of a doubt that their children are well and loved. Walking the path of a grieving parent isn't easy. No one can completely understand what this experience is like for you because it is a personal path. Those of us who have not walked this path can offer love and a listening ear as people find their footing in an entirely new world.

Opening the conversation about grief and talking constructively about it is a step I hope will come soon. This has been taboo for far too long, and it only serves to keep people in pain. I wish for you peace in your healing journey and that you take what you have learned and share it with others. As you heal, we all heal. These are the gifts of the soul.

CHAPTER

Five

Soul Puppy
by Dr. Colleen Brown DVM

DR. COLLEEN BROWN DVM

Dr. Colleen Brown is an Integrative Veterinarian, Bestselling Author, Mixed Media Artist and Adjunct Professor of Biology. She resides in Phoenix, AZ with her son Tyler, Rottweiler Sam and cats Sally and Roker. She is the owner of Brown Veterinary Housecalls and Soul Puppy Holistic Healing where she offers Integrative Veterinary Medicine for dogs and cats and TCVM for horses. Dr. Brown is also the creator of Drskippyart. She paints mixed media artwork and teaches local workshops. Her art can be found in local shops and online. Her favorite subjects to paint include angels and horses, but mostly she enjoys intuitive painting. Information on her services can be found at Brownvetservices.com and soulpuppy.net.

Soul Puppy
by Dr. Colleen Brown DVM

The practice of veterinary medicine is both an art and a science. Paths within the profession are plentiful and include, but are not limited to, private practice, research, specialization, academia, emergency, exotic, shelter, zoo, holistic or integrative medicine. How a veterinarian interacts with patients, approaches cases and communicates with clients is unique to each. Having worn a multitude of hats within the profession, I have discovered, aside from being an art and a science, that veterinary medicine is also a journey.

My journey began as a little girl who knew deep within her soul that she would become a veterinarian. Like most children, I loved all animals, but horses held a special place in my heart. During veterinary school, I completed as many equine rotations and volunteer opportunities as possible. As career goals evolved, the desire to include horses in my work remained steady. My path unfolded with becoming a new doctor, both a new and single mother, and having to cope with multiple family deaths simultaneously. Pursuing small animal medicine over equine medicine seemed to be the logical choice under the circumstances. Choosing mind over heart, I safely gave my horse dreams back to my inner child for safekeeping. As difficult as this is to admit, I was also subconsciously struggling with a limiting belief that I couldn't work with horses because I didn't own one. I didn't own an iguana either, but that didn't make me feel as if pursuing exotic medicine was out of reach. Sometimes, in life, we are afraid to give ourselves the things that set our souls on fire because deep down, for whatever reason, we feel unworthy.

At the beginning of my career, when I was learning how to become a new doctor and a new mother, I started a small animal house call practice out of what I thought was a necessity. I needed a flexible schedule for my son and the freedom to help my mother as she underwent cancer treatment. After the devastating loss of both my mother and maternal grandparents the summer after graduation from veterinary school, I struggled with grief and too much responsibility on my shoulders. Overwhelmed and lacking confidence in my ability to support my son and sister, I put my house call practice on hold, except for regular patients. I then embarked on a decade of exploration within the profession.

I am grateful for the experience I gained during my years of working as an associate veterinarian, relief doctor/independent contractor, low-cost spay/neuter surgeon, hospital medical director and even adjunct professor of biology. Like any career, some positions were better than others. In hindsight, the stressful ones I endured longer than I should have. I became quite skilled at adapting to and tolerating unhealthy situations. After all, I had been in survival mode with the birth of my son during school and then the loss of my support system shortly after. Despite the stress, I did enjoy the connections I had with clients and patients, the relationships created with colleagues and the time spent teaching and learning from my students. For some reason though, I felt as if I wasn't living my truth. I was searching for a greater sense of purpose and belonging and yearned for a deeper connection with my clients and patients. I also longed for more peace and balance for myself and my family. After tolerating a corporate position, I wanted to leave the profession altogether. I was suffering from unprocessed emotions, prolonged grief, anxiety, depression, and in a sense, compassion fatigue. Ironically, despite the various hats I wore within the profession, I hadn't given myself permission to do the one thing I truly wanted—work with horses.

My unique path has been as much about healing myself as it has been about healing my patients. I have learned a lot about veterinary medicine and patient care. Yet, the self-care, healthy boundaries, finding my tribe, following the whispers of my heart, being my authentic self and incorporating spirituality into my work, are the wisdom I now treasure. From an outside perspective, these appear to have little to do with the practice of veterinary medicine. From an inside perspective, in the current climate of compassion fatigue and suicide amongst veterinarians today, these lessons can be life-changing and lifesaving. I have learned that what my soul has been craving, only I can create. Discovering my authentic self and releasing fear of judgment, mostly my own, has set me on a beautiful healing journey. I take solace in the belief that we will always be guided to where we are meant to be.

The turn of the tides did not come as one swift surge that made everything better. It was the ebb and flow of smaller waves over time, each in sync with the beat of what made my heart sing. The more I listened to my higher self, the more my life began to shift in positive ways. It started outside of work with yoga and art classes. I will never forget the first time I attended a yoga class. I cried! It was embarrassing and I was brought to tears. With each vinyasa, I began to release little bits of the pain and grief I had been carrying since the death of my mother. I had been on survival mode for a long time. There's great beauty in the simple yet powerful healing ability of gentle stretching and mindful breathing that allows for one's complete surrender.

In addition to yoga, my other savior has been art. Sometimes the healer needs healing and art heals. I listened to the whispers of my heart and enrolled in several online mixed media art classes. The act of putting paint and paper on canvas with one's hands is incredibly cathartic. I enjoy the meditative process that painting intuitively gifts the artist. Art has become an important part of my life and is part of the greater vision I have for my healing practice and creative life. I do believe it is possible to combine what sets one's soul on fire into a divine life purpose and spiritually-based career. Let go of limiting beliefs and watch how quickly dreams come to fruition.

In my quest for more meaning in my career and a deeper sense of personal fulfillment, I began learning about holistic modalities for myself and my patients. Topics such as acupuncture, herbal medicine, homeopathy, essential oils, species-specific nutrition and energy healing all resonated with me. Inspired, I attended my first out of state conference of the American Holistic Veterinary Medical Association. This is where I found my tribe. I had been to conferences and continuing education events before, but there was something magical in the air at this one. The high-vibe energy, open-heartedness of everyone I met and intangible sense of spirituality made my heart sing. The prayer before dinner in the large dining hall for all attendees brought tears to my eyes. The last time I can say I felt such an intense sense of belonging was when my mother and grandparents were still alive. A whole new world of like-minded souls and holistic pursuits opened to me. Going to this conference changed my life. I made lifelong friendships and important decisions pertaining to the next phase of my journey.

One of the best decisions I have made regarding my career and work-life balance was taking a leap of faith and enrolling in advanced training at The Chi Institute of Trad-itional Chinese Veterinary Medicine. As a single mother, this was a financial leap of faith, but one that I knew would be a blessing for my clients, patients, my family and myself. I began with the mixed practice acupuncture program because it included horses. Now that my son was older, this was my way of bringing my dream of working with horses out from the ether and into reality. The idea of working with horses as a holistic integrative veterinarian appealed to me even more than my earlier desire to work with them from a western medicine standpoint. The universe will always direct us onto the path we are meant to follow. It may not be the road or timeframe we desire, but we will get there in divine timing, nonetheless, with faith. I'm still waiting to own my first horse and I still feel some limiting beliefs, but I am learning that it is okay because it is part of the journey. I know there are horses in need of my help and holding onto limited beliefs doesn't help them or myself. Dreams are given to us because we have the power to see them through. Enrolling in The Chi Institute has helped me make that dream a reality. My long-term goal is to complete the full master's degree program in Traditional Chinese Veterinary Medicine and become a Certified Practitioner.

Traditional Chinese Veterinary Medicine (TCVM) is an ancient practice grounded in Chinese Daoist philosophy. It has been used in China to treat animals for thousands of years and is an adaptation of Traditional Chinese Medicine (TCM) used to treat humans. Regarded as a more holistic approach than Western medicine, this ancient practice is backed by modern research. The four main branches of TCVM include Acupuncture, Herbal Medicine, Food Therapy and Tui Na. Concepts such as Qi, Yin Yang, and the Five Element Theory play an important role in pattern diagnosis and treatment of patients.

The first branch of TCVM, acupuncture, consists of the insertion of sterile needles into acupoints found along meridians of the body allowing for the movement of Qi, the life-force energy. Herbal Medicine utilizes herbal ingredients of various blends to treat disease patterns. Food therapy treats and prevents imbalances with diet via concepts such as taste and energetics. Tui Na is a form of medical massage used to promote the circulation of Qi and restore balance.

The Yin Yang Theory pertains to the concept that everything can be divided into opposite aspects. For example, masculine and feminine, light and dark, hot and cold. All yang has Yin parts and all Yin has Yang parts. Yin is associated with night, winter, old, chronic, quiet, cold, introvert and female. Yang is associated with day, summer, bright, active, hot, acute, young, strong, extrovert and male. Animals can have Yin and Yang constitutions or personalities. A Yin animal may be quiet, shy, aloof, and prefer warmth. A Yang animal may be hyperactive, outgoing, dominant, and prefer a cool environment.

The Five Element Theory in Traditional Chinese Veterinary Medicine is the concept generated from ancient observation where seasons, elements, and organs of the body are in constant motion and have a functional relationship with one another. The five elements consist of fire, earth, metal, water and wood. When the elements are in balance, there is harmony. Fire feeds the earth which creates ore for metal that can be made into tools to collect water that is used to nourish wood. When there is imbalance there is dis-ease. Fire melts the metal which chops the wood that dams the earth and stops the flow of water. Each unique element and constitution are associated with different parameters and traits. Some of the parameters include season, climate, color, flavor and emotion, to name a few. People and animals share characteristics within the different elements, but each of us has our unique constitution or personality. Fire, for example, is associated with summer, heat, bitter foods, the color red and the emotion of joy. The organs associated with the fire element are the heart and pericardium. Animals with a fire constitution are easily excited, friendly, playful and vocal. This constitution may be prone to disease of the heart or shen. In TCVM, shen is the mind which is housed in the heart, therefore, it is not uncommon for animals of this constitution to suffer from behavioral issues or separation anxiety.

Earth is associated with late summer, damp, yellow, sweet and worry. Associated organs include the spleen and stomach. An animal with an earth constitution is laid back, easy going, friendly and slow moving. Imbalances for animals within this element include excessive worry, obesity and gastrointestinal disease.

Metal is associated with fall, white, pungent tastes and sadness. The organs associated with metal include the lung and large intestines. The metal constitution is an animal that is aloof, independent, likes order and rules, and is quiet. An unbalanced metal gets upset with change, is prone to sadness, grief, depression and lung disease.

Water is associated with winter, cold, grey or black, salty taste and fear. Organs include the kidney and bladder. A water personality tends to be timid, shy, fearful, nervous, and may bite. Unbalanced, this constitution is prone to total withdrawal, renal disease, arthritis and premature aging.

Wood is associated with spring, wind, green, sour and anger. Organs consist of the liver and gall bladder. Personality traits include dominance, aggression, confidence, athleticism and fearlessness. Imbalances in this element include irritability, anger, growling and biting, kicking, tendon and ligament issues, liver and biliary disease, eye problems and seizures.

Incorporating TCVM into my toolbox of healing modalities has allowed me to help my patients on a completely new level, foster the deeper sense of purpose and connection I was searching for and officially begin my equine practice. In addition to gaining new knowledge to help my patients, I have also learned an incredible amount about myself. After studying the Five Element Theory, I learned that my unique constitution is metal. All the years filled with prolonged grief, coupled with bouts of respiratory disease when stressed now make sense, as does my ability to get along or not with different constitutions. Some of my best friends are wood and so are some of my enemies. It's all about balance. If a wood or fire is unbalanced, look out, especially when dealing with animals. Life makes more sense within the Five Element Theory. It's fun too. Clients love to discern their pet's unique constitution along with their own.

I feel extremely fulfilled now that I can offer integrative medicine to my patients and I know this is the beginning of my holistic journey. I am making a difference in the lives of both my patients and their owners while continuing to heal myself. I have come full circle. I now know that the house call practice I started all those years ago was not out of necessity, but rather something that suits me and my need for freedom to be myself in both my career and personal life. I recently took another leap of faith with the opening of my TCVM healing room. I now embrace my uniqueness and vision for the future. In a sense, I feel as if my journey has just begun. I am not just a veterinarian—I am a healer.

I dedicate this book to all the horses who have been patiently waiting for me to step into my purpose. Thank you to my family, friends, mentors, pets, clients, patients and students.

"It does not matter how slowly you go, as long as you do not stop." Chinese Proverb

CHAPTER

Six

Your Life, Your Truth
And Words To Live By
by Debra Rohrer

DEBRA K. ROHRER

Debra K. Rohrer is the owner/founder of Solutions 4 Life, a strategic consulting and coaching business based in Scottsdale, AZ. She's recognized as a creative, intuitive, strategic planner and effective problem solver. She is a featured author in the book, *When I Rise, I Thrive*. Through consultation, she guides her clients as they reach their visions of what they want to achieve. Debra has over 25 years of experience in strategic consulting and coaching, life transition coaching, addiction recovery coaching, career and educational consulting and entrepreneurial consulting. When not helping people, she loves spending time with her family. Debra earned a B.S. in Business from Arizona State University and graduated from the Southwest Institute of Healing Arts as a Certified Transformational Life Coach. She is currently completing her M.S. in Psychology at Grand Canyon University. Debra is available for strategic consulting, coaching and speaking. To connect with her, visit www.solutions4lifecoaching.com or contact her at 602-882-0038 and debbie@solutions4lifecoaching.com.

Acknowledgments

Thank you for your unending support: Chip Hickey, Erika Hickey, Bob Rohrer, Marge Rohrer, Alex Lovisetto, Beth Lovisetto, Christopher Lovisetto, Rob Rohrer, Carla Rohrer, Michael Rice and Leona Young.

Your Life, Your Truth
And Words To Live By
by Debra K. Rohrer

Introduction

D o you sometimes experience a sense of looking straight into the vast unknown of your future and it doesn't fill you with hope, but of being overwhelmed and fearful?

When you finish reading this chapter, I want you to come back to this introduction and make a written list of ten of your personal truths. These are the words you live by in your life. I'm a Strategic Consultant, helping people with business and life strategies. I find that my clients don't know what they think about those things. They've never formulated, "This is what I believe. This is my truth. This is what moves me through my life."

To give you an idea of the kind of personal truths you need to write down, here are three of ten that I wrote down when I was going through a difficult time:

- Find your highest, overarching purpose and cherish it.
- Tell people they are special, amazing and that you love them.
- Ask something greater than yourself for help, constantly.

After you have ten written down, ask yourself, "What am I going to do with it?" Have you ever made a list of priorities and it fell flat? You felt like it's a whirlwind and you're overwhelmed again, thinking, "What direction am I going?"

After you've identified your personal truths, you've got to truly own them. How do you do that? Start with action. Before we get to that, let me ask you: once you have such a list, do you follow up with yourself? Can you self-motivate, gauge where you are and see if you're making progress? You may have to enlist someone to help.

I've become unmotivated on occasion and I couldn't see how to get out. My immediate reaction was, "I need to find someone who can help me see how I'm doing with my action steps. It is okay if I don't do my step, but let's figure out why I don't do it. Did something change in my sight that needs to shift? Do I need to tweak the goal? What on my path is getting in my way? I'm not going to stay stuck."

The most amazing thing about my journey is that each experience along the way has been a life lesson, one that I cradle in my hands and feel in my heart, a treasured piece of this beautiful mosaic I call my life. Let me show you how to find the same pieces in your life.

Emerging New Life

Let's revisit the question that I asked at the beginning: do you sometimes experience a sense of looking straight into the vast unknown of your future and it doesn't fill you with hope, but of being overwhelmed and fearful?

I'm going to be honest with you. When I was asked by the publisher to write a chapter for this book, I said, "Absolutely. I'll do it." Later, I realized, "Oh my gosh. I'm overwhelmed in my life right now. I have this, that, and the other thing going on. If I had the time, I'd do it, but why in the world did I say I would? How am I going to fit this in and also get my other life and career obligations done?"

In times like this, we feel like we're standing still. Visions of what was and what will not be pass by your consciousness in horrifying and exhilarating (but not exciting) ways. The first thing I did was realize that this "middle space" I was in, that you may be in right now, is a transition space. It's not purgatory. It's not like a vacuum of nothingness. It's a place where you're moving.

I find that most people struggle to break down their middle space into separated parts that they can identify. They'll come to me and think it is one problem, but it's something completely different or they're layered on top of each other. It may be a mind, body and spirit separation, but more often, it's along the lines of work, spirituality, family, health and exercise.

Being in the middle space is about letting go and being fully present. By doing this, it won't be so horrifying to take a step forward. You'll start to see what scares you or challenges you. This is where dreams and goals formulate. This validates where you are at that exact moment. Instead of feeling, "I'm just wandering, I don't know where I am," you realize that if you persist and work at it, this is a purposeful place to be.

Take charge of your middle space. Assemble it. Be mindful about it. Consult with others about what you're finding. Set some goals. Write them down. Stay centered in your middle space. Let go. These things will propel you forward to keep going. Forward-moving actions start with forward-thinking. Bring what you need prior to being in this middle space; let go of the rest.

Freedom to See

Does your life often feel so hard that the only option is to take flight?

In the previous section, we talked about your emerging new life. That was mostly about owning where you are and being mindful of where you can potentially go. This is about letting yourself slow down at that moment. It's about the freedom to see clearly. It's about *how* to see. It's about looking intensely.

How are you supposed to do that when you're stressed, and the one thing you don't want to do is slow down because you're sure you'll give up? It's about constant motion, not about how fast you're moving.

How do you notice what's around you? Do you notice a little bird pecking at leftover food on the sidewalk as you walk by? We completely miss our lives when we don't slow down. So Stop. Notice the shape of the branches on the nearby tree. Feel the breeze. Connect with your life. Where are you now in this moment? Look at the people you're with and sense their presence. Enjoy their presence. Allow the disassembly of your world to bring you to a place of heightened awareness about every single thing that touches your being.

Most people are running from themselves or from something in their lives. They're not present in the now. Their minds are constantly thinking ahead. If you focus on the details of the moment, you end up appreciating the tangibility of what you're seeing and visualizing; the taste and textures of life and things.

You give meaning to the moment. When you're overwhelmed and you don't slow down so that you can pay attention to your surroundings, you miss it. The reason you're feeling like you want to get away from everything in your life is because you're not paying attention to the small things. You're not paying attention to your life as it is happening. All the things that are valuable to you are passing by. This is the benefit of slowing down when you're overwhelmed. This is how your life will change for the better.

Love, Kindness and Hope

Have you ever let yourself cry to the point of sounding like a wounded animal because of your sadness, sense of loss and grief just riveting through your entire being?

Have you ever felt this way? I have. We feel like that because change is powerful and because we're going through a lot of changes in our lives and they're taking us somewhere we didn't imagine. Probably, that's somewhere scary. It could be a great place you've never imagined and that's why you feel this way, but a lot of times, it's not a great place; it's a stressful place, an anxious place. It can also be a place of opportunity. Let every fiber of your being and the raw emotion you've created carry a message of courage and excitement about the world and everyone in it.

CHAPTER

Seven

The Healing Journey
by Dina Gilmore

DINA GILMORE

Dina F. Gilmore (aka *She Who Heals Plenty* or *Ashwani*) is a certified Shamanic Practitioner, Licensed Massage Therapist, Reiki Master Teacher, Photographer, Filmmaker, Scriptwriter, Broadcaster, Podcaster and Best-Selling author of "When I Rise, I Thrive." She is a Southerner who grew up in Texas. In 2012, she moved to Colorado to thrive in a more diverse state and build community connections. Dina created Mobile Shaman to share the healing art of Shamanism across the country in our modern-day society. She leads Shamanic Journey Circles, stories I heard, "I was not good enough, there is too much competition, I will never make it, make your art a hobby and get a real career-paying job." I let stories crush my dreams. I packed up all my supplies, sold my drawing table, and left my art degree in the dust because I believed what I heard.

In Shamanic medicine, I had what you would call a "soul loss" from multiple instances in my life. Soul loss is where a piece of your spirit or soul checks out and leaves because that part no longer feels safe. Abuse and traumatic events set the scene for this type of loss to occur. I had lost parts of myself I never imagined would return, starting with early childhood. The old stories combined with coming out as gay in the latter part of my teens were unbearable, and I overdosed on everything in my medicine cabinet, washed down with wine coolers to end my suffering. The words, "I don't know if we can save your daughter" burned in my mind as I became semi-coherent. I felt jolted awake witnessing the tears streaming down my momma's face and holding my hand with profound sadness in her eyes which I never want to see again. That was the defining moment that changed my life, and I verbally made a pact with God that I would always work on myself and with other people because he saved me from myself. I sought a professional counselor to start sharing my past and gave myself permission to heal. My self-permission gave me a realization that I no longer wanted to work in sales. I recalled a childhood dream of wanting to make a grander impact in the world. I registered into massage therapy school in 1999, and that began my healer journey.

Your healing journey is yours to experience, so paying close attention to how you are being in the moment is a vital key to your progression. I have learned the hard way to think before I act. My old stories defined every romantic relationship in my past. I automatically engaged in them thinking, "What's the point? You are going to leave me anyway because of my childhood abandonment instances." No woman ever had a chance of keeping me present in the relationship because I had to break down the programming of the ghosts of my past. I would visualize my perfect partner, but the wheels constantly turned with me thinking that I was not worthy, and I would self-sabotage.

In 2014, a massage client of mine introduced me to Landmark Education for personal and professional development. I arrived late to the special evening because of work and timidly walked into a room filled with close to two hundred people. My client had saved a front row seat for me. She knew me well and that I could not sit passively in the back and not receive what I was there to attain. She believed in me and took a stand for what could be possible in my life. That was the best light-bulb moment when the Forum Leader wrote twenty-five areas of life on the chalkboard where this work could greatly improve my life. What stood out to me the most were relationships, love, career, finances and sex. I registered that night, took their courses for the next three years and tremendously improved my life. The past stories still surface occasionally, but now I choose to use my voice, communicate freely and utilize my healing toolbox to take actions, even if fear is present. I choose to act from a place of love, and not react from heightened emotions. That was a monumental shift for me. I am a firm believer in finding what works best for you since no two people are the same. Embracing the willingness to look within, being vulnerable with yourself, and asking what is not working, leads you closer to self-discovery. Being a healer, we ask this of clients, and we need to be willing to ask that of ourselves. Embrace these healing words when working with clients or when working with yourself.

Elemental Healing

May the wind carry away your pain,
May the Earth heal all wounds,
May the water cleanse your body,
May the fire breathe passion into your soul to carry on your journey to healing!
So be it! Aho! – Dina F. Gilmore

Questions to ask yourself:

- What is not working that I would like to alter, change or replace with new action?
- Am I willing to dive deep within myself?
- Am I willing to listen to my heart and soul?
- Will I be willing to give love to myself first? Even airlines tell you to put the oxygen mask on yourself before assisting others. Be courageous and put that oxygen mask on!
- How am I being in this moment?
- Are these my true emotions? If so, where are they coming from? A helpful hint is to be fully present with yourself and free from distractions.
- Will I give myself permission and make conscious choices to heal?
- Am I ready?

Empowering words to inspire your journey:

- I am my greatest potential, so I choose to create the masterpiece of me!
- Treat every day as a new day!
- Effective communication removes conflict!
- Communication is a foundation needed for any healthy relationship!
- I believe in me! I believe in me! I believe in me!
- I have the power to start a new beginning with myself from this moment forward!
- I am the author of my story, and I write where my character goes!
- I choose to live my life from a place of love!
- I choose my actions toward the ideal situation or outcome for myself!
- The more I learn about myself, the greater my healing process!
- I will do for myself as I do for others!
- The most important relationship is the one with oneself!
- I am already succeeding because I am taking action toward a goal.
- "Your vision will become clear only when you look into your heart," is one of my favorite quotes by Carl Jung.

Dina's healing guidance:

- Stay calm, take a deep breath and get present. Take another deep breath. One more.
- Think before you act.
- Ask yourself, what is important to me?
- Routinely cleanse your mind, body, spirit and soul selves. My favorites are soaking in a warm salt

Facebook.com/ElizabethHarbinEventPage

Acknowledgments:

Without question, I must thank the following individuals for helping me through one of the most difficult yet rewarding times of my life. My tribe: Linda Ballesteros, Jenny Cabaniss, Luann Morris, Heidi Frazier, Wendy McDonald, Laura Beikman, Sandra Crosswell, Tonda Frazier, Foxye Jackson, Xotchil Garibay, Kristin Parker, Cindy Childress, Lynn Hendrix, Myla Patton and my soul family brother, Mario Ballesteros. My brother, Bob Harbin, my family, and of course my biggest fan and champion, my mother, Eleanor Rhodes.

Failure to Self-Destruct
By Elizabeth Harbin

Failure to Self-Destruct was the book title that my mother, Eleanor Rhodes, had come up with back in 1981. She intended to write a book based on how she had survived so many setbacks in her life without self-imploding. She was only 46 at that time. She was proud of the fact that, as a single parent, she had survived raising two children, lived through three husbands, survived cancer, remained in touch with lifelong friends and her family was still intact.

By her 40's, she had gone through major back surgery and was a uterine cancer survivor; however, her greatest achievement was becoming a nonsmoker. Her partying days and wild child ways were fading fast, and she needed to have passion return to her life again. Fortunately, she discovered Oprah, Deepak Chopra, Dr. Wayne W. Dyer, Thomas A. Harris, M.D., Louise Hay, Andrew Weil, M.D., Unity church and goddess retreats.

One of the first healing modalities she learned about was Reiki. Reiki is pronounced "Ray-Key" and is a technique used for stress reduction and relaxation that also promotes healing. It is administered by "laying on hands" and is based on the idea that an unseen life force energy flows through us and is what causes us to be alive. If one's life force energy is low, then we are more likely to get sick or feel stress, and if it is high, we are more capable of being happy and healthy. Since she had received several Reiki treatments from her many goddess retreat weekends, she knew the power it held, and she knew it worked because it worked on her!

Not only did Reiki improve her depression, but she discovered it also helped her back pain, which was becoming chronic. The idea of being able to receive that kind of energy and direct it to a single point on one's body for healing was fascinating. She started writing down prayers for all of her friends in need, and would hold them in her hands and say prayers over her writings. In cleaning out some of her notebooks and journals after her death, I found a prayer she had written 30 years ago for one of her dear friends. Sure enough, that prayer had been answered.

Let's flash-forward to January 2018, when Mother was 83. By this time, I had moved in with her and became her full-time caregiver. There had been a long running joke between my mother and me. She would say, "You know, I'm not going to be around much longer," and I would say, "You can't go yet, your insurance policy is not paid up." She would look at me with those Eleanor eyes, and by this time, I had learned to shoot them right back to her. She would get tickled, and we would break into laughter.

But now, her brilliant mind was forgetting the simplest of tasks. Before our worlds had shrunken to being homebound full-time, I became a Reiki master. Of course, having access to Reiki treatments from her daughter any time of the day or night was like winning the lottery. When she fell and broke her ankle, which resulted in two surgeries and rehab stays, I would visit and give her a Reiki treatment. The practice of Reiki doesn't only help the one receiving— it also knows what the sender needs.

Unfortunately, even after her recovery, her falls continued. Her Chronic Obstructive Pulmonary Disease (COPD) and asthma became more prevalent, as she started having panic attacks that would shut off her windpipe. Each time she had one of those events, I would use Reiki energy on her back and move up to her lungs and throat to help relax her enough to catch that one big breath.

We tried everything to help elevate her mood. We treated her room like a vacation suite and not a place of confinement. Her friends brought her beautiful linens and comforters. One time, there were so many pillows on her bed it took almost 15 minutes to change the pillowcases. She loved having her pillows Reiki-energized and often said it helped her sleep better.

I tried to keep her life as positive as possible, but her decline also brought out another side of her personality. There were times she would become hateful and vicious. She could cut you to the heart with laser-precision. To not take her comments personally was a task I failed at many times. Sure, I pushed back when I could, but I thought I was the caregiver and had to take it and go on.

Resentment would settle in if I did not do something about it. I knew that if my anger was left untreated, I would explode and say hurtful things which would serve no purpose. It is amazing how much I had forgotten about the ways of the Reiki practitioner when I was in the thick of caregiving. I forgot how Reiki releases emotional wounds, improves concentration, and helps change negative conditioning and behavior. It also reduces the impact of stress physically, emotionally, mentally and energetically. How could I have forgotten all of that?

The other part of being in the caregiver situation is that we shut off parts of our brain so that we can survive. That includes self-care information and knowledge. So I began saying the prayer created by Dr. Usui every morning:

"Just for today, I will not worry. Just for today, I will not be angry. Just for today, I will be kind to every living thing. Just for today, I will be thankful for all my blessings. Just for today, I will do my work honestly. Just for today, I will be compassionate and forgiving. Just for today, I will find joy in even the smallest of life's gifts. Just for today, I will feel at peace." Also, in my prayer, I added, "Just for today, I know I have the proper people helping me."

We had two nurses come to our house to introduce themselves as Mother's new replacements, and they suggested to move Mother to rehab to build up her core and save my back. Her legs were useless by this time. Once in rehab, however, her decline spiraled rapidly. Getting her core strength was not going to happen. The days were clicking by, and it was getting closer for her to come home. How was I going to take care of her at home in her condition?

You may or may not know the feeling of being so overwhelmed that you have no words or thoughts, so you create no action. Fortunately, Linda, my friend for over 20 years whose husband passed after being in hospice, stepped in and suggested I call Mother's new nurses and tell them the situation. The next day, I got a call from hospice. A calming voice said she would take care of everything and be at my house the next day. I let my brother know and asked Linda to be our ears for what this hospice coordinator had to say.

Inviting Linda was a good idea because I only heard, "Get rid of your mom's king-sized bed by tomorrow, get the burial service set up so that Mother could be picked up at the proper time, and then, we will let nature take its course." What did that mean? Fortunately, Linda had heard every word, remembered all the details we needed to know and what to prepare for. The hospice bed arrived the following day.

Trying to find a crematory or burial service under normal circumstances is stressful, but when it's got to be done right away—it's awful. Prices ranged from $6,000–$10,000, or higher. I said my prayer and this time I added, "I can't do this alone." Within 30 minutes, I had a phone number a name and the nicest man I had ever spoken to. The cost was less than half of other quoted prices, and all he wanted me to do was go back and sit with my mother and call him when I needed him. Did that Reiki prayer work or what?

By Saturday, June 16th, 2018, Mother had been home for seven days. She had new medications and was getting them every six hours. I could no longer leave the house unless someone I trusted stayed with her. People were coming in and out of the house at all hours. Food was being delivered. Supplies from hospice, nurses, and phone calls became controlled chaos. Several of Mother's closest friends visited unexpectedly because they had a feeling they needed to see her one more time.

CHAPTER

Nine

You Are Love
by Virginia "Ginger" Adams

VIRGINIA "GINGER" ADAMS

Virginia "Ginger" Adams – Master Energy Healer, Intuitive Mentor, Published Author and Creator of the *Universal Gravity Code Program*. Virginia is a well-known motivator, medical practice administrator and a featured author in the internationally best-selling book "52 Weeks of Gratitude Journal". Her dedication, integrity, and intuitive field; they felt a calling. I was in Medical Practice Administration, and for some reason, I had been placed into their lives. As an employee of physicians and a supervisor of nurses, physicians and therapists, it was my honor to support them, but I saw these providers as the "empowered" ones. I also realized that "healers" tend not to be good at self-care. They give their heart and soul to others, often depleting themselves. From this perspective, the idea of "Heal the healer" began to resonate with me and my purpose began to reveal.

Though I struggled with the acceptance of my newly given mandate, I watched my life path begin to change. I call that time "the duality of Ginger." On one side, I remained a focused administrator, but there was another spiritual side of me that began to expand. Through that expansion, I began to study alternative healing modalities. I became certified in a few different methods, but I still did not act upon my new knowledge. Fear still held me back, and I felt paralyzed to practice these methods or embrace the idea of publicly being a healer.

Why Did I Step Into the Power of Being a Healer? Reconnective Healing!

During this time of exploration, my world was rocked by a process referred to as "The Reconnection and Reconnective Healing." I became inimitably aware that it is possible to share healing frequencies from one person to another just by walking past, sitting by, thinking of or placing my attention on another living being. I do not have to touch them and they do not have to be aware of the interaction.

I discovered that the Reconnective Healing Frequencies connect us to a place of perfect balance, where we can allow ourselves to be led to what is needed to return to wholeness. This is how I could heal the healers! This is how I could assist the healing of whoever came to me!

Once we are attuned to a higher frequency, we walk, talk, sleep and exist in it. This is our divine connection, our sharing in the perfection and magnificence of the Creative Force, our Orenda. All that we have to do is wake up and remember.

We hear a lot about finding and following our life purpose or spiritual calling. For most of us, these ideas are preceded and followed by huge question marks. How do I know? Who is going to tell me? What if I don't hear it right? What if I don't know how? Who is going to show me? What if my mom (family and friends) disapproves? Where does this knowledge come from? And on and on and on.

My current path as a healer is a demonstration of me finally following my life purpose. But from time to time, the question marks come flooding back in. How do I know who is going to support me financially as I skip down this lovely little path? Who and what appointed me to this purpose? And my all-time favorite: is this just my imagination?

These questions led me to look up the word "purpose" in the thesaurus. These are some of the words I found: drive, determination, resolution, persistence, perseverance, tenacity, single-mindedness.

I've discovered I have them all when it comes to my energy healing practice. As for single-mindedness, I choose *love*—period—end of story. My call to action as a healer could be described as "A Warrior of Love." I honor this calling by facilitating Reconnective Healing®, The Reconnection®, intuitive mentoring and through my writing. I am now living my purpose.

What about you? What will you allow yourself to imagine? How does it hold up to the above question marks? If you find yourself questioning your purpose, use your imagination to create a story in which you are determined, resolved, persistent, and with great perseverance and tenacity. Imagine a story where you are single-minded towards a dream and a reason to exist.

Get busy putting check marks by your question marks. Step by beautiful step, you will glide down your life purpose path. You too have been called to love, called to your unique form of healing. Realize your innate abilities. Let go of any fear holding you back. Once you allow yourself to be who you truly are, you will walk in love every single day.

If you are reading this, you are ready to wake up and remember. To help you along your way, make a photocopy of this section or write it down, cut it out, laminate it and put it in your back pocket. Keep it handy, just in case you forget who you truly are:

- You are made of light, nothing more nothing less.
- Within the light are energy and information. This energy, light and information is who you are in your infinite connection to pure love.
- You are not your physical body or emotional body. They are just an illusion of this time and space. The body is something to look past or

transcend from, using the lessons the body may bring.

- Enlightenment is the transcendence of our human bodies and the remembrance of our true nature, which is light and love.
- You are *love*, not made of love, not experiencing love, not sharing love—you are *love*.
- You are the voice within, the knowing which has no beginning and no end.
- You are a divine being, connected to your Source, or what I call, God.
- Our Source is omnipotent, omniscient, omnipresent and omnibenevolent.
- The vastness of the Universe and the Universes beyond cannot begin to corral the essence which you share with your Source. You are an infinite being connected to all.
- "Heal yourself" is remembering that we are not our body. Self-healing is the allowance of our inner knowing to embrace and embody our divine and intrinsic perfection and magnificence.
- *You are love.*

CHAPTER

Ten

Essential Oils For Healing
by Ginger Parrack

GINGER PARRACK

Ginger Parrack is a certified mind, body and spirit practitioner who came into this world knowing all that is around her and connecting with loved ones on the other side of the veil. She combines channeled intuitive messages and insight with her healing sessions. Ginger's spirit guides work in conjunction with her clients' guides. Together they collectively assist in releasing that which no longer serves them on many levels. Ginger is a certified psychic/medium and spiritual advisor trained at Lisa William's LWISSD. Her hands-on healing and holistic practices consist of over 200 hours of training in Western/Eastern Reflex-ology, Auricular Therapy, Western herbalism and flower essences. She is a Certified Clinical Aromatherapist, Reiki Master and crystal healer. Ginger has dedicated her life to her healing practices. She has an extensive background in the medical field as a Registered Nurse, working from new life to assisting in transitions to the other side in death.

Website: www.healingheartcreations.com

www.healingheartmedium.com Phone:623-476-1861,

Email: ginger@healingheartcreations.com

ginger@healingheartmedium.com

Acknowledgments

First, I would like to thank Kyra Schaefer and As You Wish Publishing for encouraging me to share my knowledge. Secondly, I want to thank my loving Husband Brad Parrack for believing in me, supporting me and understanding and accepting my weirdness regardless. To all of my mentors in the Aromatherapy industry ie: David Crow, L.Ac, Kurt Schnaubelt, PH.D. and Andrea Butje. For my friend, mentor and flower sister Rhonda PallasDowney for teaching me the voices of flower essences and the medicine behind them. Thank you to all of my spiritual family for the support over the years. Special thank you to my Lilydale sisters for all of your love and support. To my spiritual mentor Lisa Williams psychic/medium, for pushing me out of my comfort zone I will be forever grateful. To my Mom for always knowing I was different than my siblings, encouraging me to be my best and never doubting me. Miss you.

Essential Oils For Healing
by Ginger Parrack

If you are reading this book, then you are searching for answers, looking for like-minded people or looking for answers as to why you never felt like you belonged with those around you. For as long as I can remember, I wanted to help people and animals feel better. I wanted to ease their pain and suffering. I could see and feel their pain. I could walk into a room of people and know who was suffering emotionally, physically or spiritually. It wasn't until I was in my late teens that I realized the average person could not do this. I cared and wanted to help and make a difference. So the search began to find a career or job that allowed me to walk my path.

My first choice was to be a veterinarian. Then, I realized I could not euthanize animals without feeling their souls leave and crying my eyes out. So my next choice was to be a nun and travel the world to help others, but I realized that wouldn't work for me. So I decided to work in the medical field as a Registered Nurse. Nurses were the original healers, the medicine women, the midwives, the sages and herbalists. I have assisted babies with their first breath and my patients with their last breath and everyone else in between.

After working in the medical field for over 15 years, I decided there had to be a better way to help people heal on all levels. Watching physicians give patients a quick fix pill was not a solution. I could see their emotional, physical and spiritual pain. They kept coming back for medicine with no overall results. I began to search for alternative healing modalities.

Healing modalities can be learned either in a classroom or online. I have researched for hours to find the ones that piqued my interest. As an RN, I found that many modalities that were available in the European medical field were not recognized in the United States' medical community. Alternative medicine was viewed as something people wasted their money on and was not considered "real" medicine.

My RN colleagues were using "Healing Touch" with their patients. Some hospitals listed it as an alternative, free service that you could receive while hospitalized to speed your healing process. I found Reiki. This was the first healing modality that resonated with me. It was more than Healing Touch for me. This is where I discovered that if I touched people or hovered above them, I could feel where their pain was, see their energy rising off of their bodies and connect with their spirits and hear their stories. This was also when I realized that I could see spirits other than those connected to me.

With the study of Reiki, I learned to apply crystals to the body to amplify healing. Using stones to heal the body required learning about the chakras and how different stones interacted with them. Who knew that, as a child, gathering rocks would turn into healing in the future? Working with crystals required learning how to feel their energy, use them and apply them to the Reiki sessions. Seeing the results and hearing back from people I worked with encouraged me to keep looking for ways I could enhance my sessions.

Excited to learn more, I began to study Western herbalism. Initially, my first use of herbal medicine was on my dog. He had congestive heart failure, and I was searching for alternative ways to ease his suffering. I researched herbs and found some that were safe for dogs and started giving the herbs to him. When I took him to the vet for a follow up visit, the veterinarian could not believe how good he looked and asked me what I had been doing. Seeing those results sparked my passion to learn more. Eighteen months later, I had completed a certificate in Western herbalism. I learned to make my own tinctures, salves and healing ointments.

In herbalism, aromatherapy and flower essences, you are taught the "doctrine of signatures" of each plant; its healing powers and their uses (homeopathic, essential oils and medicine). To quote my teacher/mentor, Rhonda Pallas Downey, "The doctrine of signatures states that the personality and characteristics of a plant are the statement about its medicinal qualities and properties." The plant's signature is all-encompassing of its roots, leaves, stem and flower and describes where the plant thrives. Does it like cold or hot? Dark places or sunny, warm places? What kind of soil does it grow in? All of this and more gives the plant its medicine.

Aromatherapy was next on the list to learn. My goal was to be able to teach my patients and clients how to use aromatherapy to heal on a physical, emotional and spiritual level. I researched it and took every class and read every book on it that I could get my hands on. Aromatherapy resonated with me at my deepest level.

Where to Buy Essential Oils

So let's talk about aromatherapy and how to buy your essential oils (EO). Several companies are selling essential oils. I encourage you to find your oils from a reputable company. You need to ask where they source their oils from. Is it organic, unadulterated and ethically gathered? Do they believe in replacing what they take from the planet? Do your research. Look for a company with integrity. Essential oils are a gift from the earth. Let's treat them as such.

Safety with Essential Oils

I cannot emphasize enough the need for essential oil safety. Your skin is the largest organ in your body, and its absorption rate is extremely effective. These precious gifts are highly concentrated and should be used sparingly. The oils need to be diluted in carrier oil, almond, coconut, olive oil, or any other oil that is safe on the skin. They can also be added to unscented lotion.

The only two essential oils that are safe to apply directly to the skin are lavender and tea tree—all others should be diluted. Also, remember that oil and water do not mix. Ingestion of essential oils alone or in water is not recommended since many oils are volatile and can burn the sensitive mucous membranes. In France, the practice is to add the oils to a mix of ingredients before ingesting. Again, I encourage you to do the research yourself and learn the safe application of essential oils. Keep your EO in a cool, dry place for a better shelf life.

The elderly, pregnant women, children and pets are highly sensitive to essential oils and will need further dilution for safety. Some essential oils are not safe for children and pets. Essential oils can be toxic to cats. Please be careful with diffusing essential oils in the room with children and pets. Photosensitivity can occur with citrus oils. When used in the sun, they can burn your skin. Be very careful to not get Essential oils in your eyes. If you do get essential oils in your eyes then contact poison control or your physician immediately. According to the essential oil safety guidelines you may use vegetable oil (olive or coconut). Place the vegetable oil on a tissue and gently wipe the eye area. Another safety concern is that rosemary EO should not be used with anyone with a history of epilepsy or seizures. If you are interested in learning more about essential oil safety, I highly recommend *Essential Oil Safety by Robert Tisserand and Rodney Young.*

Carrier Oils, Lotions or Salts

There are many different carrier oils you can use to blend your EO in. Common carrier oils I use are jojoba, apricot or fractionated coconut oil. I try not to use nut oils to avoid allergies with my clients. Keep the oils in a cool, dry place. You can also add essential oils to salts and Epsom salts for baths.

How to Choose and Connect with Your Essential Oils

Now that I have covered most of the essentials about essential oils, let's talk about how to choose your oils and make a blend. This is the fun part. I have found that following these guidelines results in amazing blends that work for you or your client.

Practice calming your mind. Meditate, listen to music or take a walk. Find that peaceful moment to sit and take a breath. Take your time to sit with yourself in a quiet space.

Allow your thoughts to calm down so that you can feel and hear what is in your highest good. Stay in your quiet place. Have a notebook and pen with you.

Choose your oil. Pick the first one you see or that resonates with you, or for more fun, work with a friend and have them choose the oil for you. This is the preferred method as it allows you to experience the EO without any bias or previous knowledge. Take a few deep breaths. Close your eyes and imagine a beautiful white light coming into the top of your head, passing through your body, coming out of the bottom of your feet, draining all of the negative energy and stress from your body.

Apply one drop to either a cotton ball, Q-tip or a Kleenex. Close your eyes, wave the drop of EO under your nose, back and forth. If this is for a client, have them do the same. Smell the EO, first with both nostrils, then close one nostril and smell with the right side, then the left. Notice that by doing this, it will smell different. You are stimulating the right and left side of the brain. As we know, they operate differently. Don't try to guess what the oil is. You need to allow your inner knowledge to connect with the EO. While you do this, ask yourself these questions. Write down your answers.

1. Do you like or dislike the scent? Why?
2. How does it make you feel?
3. What is your first thought when you smell this oil?
4. What kind of experience does this bring up for you?
5. Describe any physical reaction you are experiencing while smelling this oil.

6. What color do you see in your mind's eye when you smell it?
7. Do you feel a particular place in your body react when you smell it?
8. Does smelling this oil evoke any memories for you? Describe them.
9. What does it smell like to you?
10. Do you like the place this oil has taken you? Can you describe it?
11. If this oil had a message for you, what would that be?
12. How did you like this smelling experience?

This is one of the most eye-opening, experiential exercises that I have ever found. It allows you to connect with your inner self and feel the oil. When we smell essential oils, they are highly volatile, meaning they evaporate quickly. The microscopic particles enter our nose and go immediately to our brain, olfactory system and nervous system. They absorb into our mucous membranes and bloodstream. Using these beautiful gifts can be healing on many levels.

Top, Middle and Base Notes

You may be thinking, "Why do I need to know this?" I am going to address this before you make your blend. This method teaches you how to use different essential oils in blending. A top note is the first fragrance you smell when you apply it to the skin. It is usually the most volatile, or evaporates first. The middle note or the "heart" of the fragrance can take ten to twenty minutes to fully develop,

shifting experiences. Heather is trained and certified in a number of healing modalities. She's worked as a joy guide and body whisperer for 20 years. Based in Richmond, Virginia, Heather serves clients around the world, helping them discover purpose and connect with inner truth through an unstructured and holistic approach. Learn more about her offerings, client reviews, and contact her through her website: www.HeatherVDunning.com

Acknowledgments

I send gratitude and appreciation to all my beloved clients, friends, and family who have been willing to trust in me and be vulnerable with their bodies during times of pain and suffering. Also, gratitude to my muse and beloved furry child, Romeo, who was abused, neglected and left for dead. He divinely found and chose us as his forever home and reminds me every day that forgiveness and unconditional love is not only possible, but necessary in living a joy-filled life.

A Practice in Self-Forgiveness
By Heather V. Dunning

Forgiveness Begins Within

Forgiveness is one of the most confusing concepts in our world today. On the one hand, it feels great, changes lives and heals the past. Forgiveness allows us to be present in the moment and clears a path to the future. On the other hand, we're taught little, if anything, about the practice of forgiveness—where it begins, or how to use it. That lack of awareness feeds falsehoods about forgiveness; to forgive someone else, or even ourselves, means to forget the transgression and somehow fail to learn a particular lesson or protect from future pain. When we do not remember that forgiveness is a practice and that it begins with ourselves, we get reminders in the form of physical pain or discomfort—reminders that are often ignored or misunderstood.

So Much More Than a Machine

In the 20 years that I've been working with the body, I have discovered and affirmed that chronic pain is a result of ignoring the body's innate wisdom. Your body is far wiser than your mind will ever be. However, your mind has the ability to override that wisdom, and in doing so, it robs you of the body's brilliance and the information you need to release yourself from a prison of pain, disease, and discomfort.

Are you in that Alcatraz of affliction? There's an easy way to tell: your language reveals it both when you talk to yourself and when you talk to others.

Ugh, my back is killing me! Oh man, my freaking neck is killing me, again! What could I have possibly done now to make my feet hurt this badly? They are killing me!

Let's talk about that language before you end up on the witness stand of a *Law & Order* episode.

The body's desire to get your attention is like a four-year-old tugging on a parent's sleeve. If ignored, the child's attempts to be heard can go from a light tug to a full-on temper tantrum. It can get ugly, fast.

Often times, we treat our bodies like our worst enemies, berating, badgering, and belittling even its best efforts. This creates a relationship of dysfunction, distrust, and discord. Recovering from this takes awareness, intention and time.

When was the last time you thanked your body for all it allows you to experience in this life? After all, the body is the only one who has been with you since the beginning and will carry you all the way to the end.

The union between your spirit and body is truly your first marriage. Its importance as your foundation cannot be overstated. In fact, I remind all of the couples I guide that their first marriage is to their body, and then, to their spouse. Until you have a healthy and loving first marriage, other intimate relationships are going to suffer. By loving and caring in commitment to self, you will see all your relationships benefit and transform.

A Client's Experience

Despite working with me for years, a client had always resisted practicing the forgiveness meditation on her own. One day, nearly as a last resort, she decided to try showing compassion to her painful parts and became elated with the results.

After 15 years of unsuccessful surgeries and unwanted side effects from pain medication, my client's chronic knee pain inspired her to try this alternative exercise. After only five minutes, her knee pain went from screaming to a light whisper. From this moment forward, she began speaking kindly and with appreciation to all her *talking parts*. The trust and love between her mind and body grew by leaps and bounds. This single exercise may not have cured all of life's imbalances, but it gave her hope, opening the door to pain-free possibility.

I have stood witness, time and again, as this forgiveness meditation has proven effective against acute and chronic pain caused by traumas, old and new, and of all sizes.

Personal Experience

I'm grateful to share with you that I typically don't experience chronic pain, but I've endured my fair share of acute pain. Throughout my life, I've experienced many episodes where something emotional, mental or physical happened within me or in my world, and my physical body took the brunt of it. I have chosen to use this meditation while sharing love and appreciation for those injured parts until my body returned to comfort, or at least, became more flexible, functional and willing to work with me again.

Patience was one of the key components in this acceptance, trust, and forgiveness. Part of rebuilding trust from within is being willing to accept the conditions and afflictions your body is currently experiencing. It is within this acceptance, in real time, that you can co-create a more open, cohesive, and joyful path forward.

Assessing Your Pain

Many people find it easier to understand and use this forgiveness meditation if they first create a "pain scale." This is a simple assessment tool, not an instrument of science. It's all relative and will change from day to day, or even moment to moment. That's why I recommend calibrating every time before starting the meditation.

If this stresses you in any way, don't worry about it. We're not striving for perfection, only progress. You can choose to jump right into the forgiveness meditation, bypassing the scale altogether. If you feel a little bit more flexible, a little lighter, or feel less tension and resistance after the meditation, that's an improvement towards the direction that you're wanting to go. That's success!

The first step of doing the forgiveness meditation is checking in with your body. With intention and purpose, you can identify both where your pain or discomfort is, and its intensity.

Use the pain scale from zero to ten to assess that intensity. Zero means no discomfort at all. Ten is the highest pain level. I often describe a ten as being so intense that you may feel the need to vomit, pass out, and even go to an emergency room so that people can understand clearly what a ten is.

State your number to yourself.

Forgiveness Meditation

Now that you have your number and know what area you want to focus on, lay your hands on that area if you can. If you're doing this in partnership with someone, they can lay their hands on you, and you can assist them. If it's an area of your body that's challenging for you to reach physically, you can reach it with your thoughts and intention.

What I like to do is lay my hands as close to the area as I can possibly get. Also, I focus my mind and breath on setting my intention, sending energy, unconditional love, and forgiveness to that area. Now that you've achieved that focus, you're going to go to a place inside yourself that's of the highest vibration.

Please think about unconditional love and invite forward that feeling. Visualize something you love that helps you feel unconditional love for the planet, such as something in nature. Or, envision someone you unconditionally love. Beloved pets are always a safe choice, as our relationships with animals are typically uncomplicated. Often, we can unconditionally love our pets more than our spouses or other family members. If you do choose to imagine a person, make sure no other heavy feelings are attached to that individual.

Take a moment to pull up the vibration of unconditional love by allowing your mind to think of this person, place or thing. Once you have it, take a nice, deep breath and check in to see where you feel it in your body. Every time you exhale during this exercise, you're going to release from that place of love, and you're going to pour that loving energy into the area of pain, discomfort or resistance.

If, at any point in time, these words below don't resonate, please shift them to the words that you can say authentically and sincerely to your body. I have found that sincerity is the key for the body to be willing to trust and connect after years of abuse, neglect, and disregard. Let's begin.

Take in a deep breath.

Slowly breathe out of your mouth, sending unconditional love to the place of pain. Remember to be sincere, gentle, and loving, as if you're holding and talking to a crying baby, and then start by saying:

Body, I see you. I hear you. I feel you.

I love you unconditionally and accept you fully

For everything you were

For everything you are

For everything you're still becoming.

Inhale deeply, sending love on the exhale, then say:

Body, I forgive you!

For all the pain, the ache, the discomfort,

For any sadness, disappointment or unmet expectations.

For any feelings of isolation, resentment, regret, guilt or shame

For all exhaustion I've ever experienced through you.

Inhale deeply, sending love on the exhale, then say:

Body, please forgive me for any unkind words, neglect, abuse or disregard

I've ever shown you, or allowed anyone else to show you.

Inhale deeply, sending love on the exhale, then say:

I am sincerely sorry. I did not realize how my thoughts, words, actions, patterns, and beliefs so greatly affected you.

Inhale deeply, sending love on the exhale, then say:

Please feel safe moving forward and

Trust in me to support you, love you, and listen to you

However you need and whenever you need it.

Inhale deeply, sending love on the exhale, then say:

I only ask that you please be patient with me as I learn to love and listen to you better.

Thank you, body, for all that you allow me to experience in this life.

Take one last deep breath, sending love on the exhale.

After you finish sharing these words with your body, check in once again. Determine your pain level. How much has it decreased?

What If It Doesn't Work?

If it hasn't budged and you're experiencing anger, frustration, concern, sadness, or impatience, it's okay. Pause for a moment and begin again. Be more sincere with your words, despite the discomfort. It may have been quite some time, if not the first time, since you have talked to your body in this manner.

Specificity can also assist in delving deeper into what your body may need to hear from you. For example, *I forgive you for not being able to climb the mountain, or put on my shirt, or hold my baby, or drive the car, or pour the milk*. Or simply feeling challenged in *standing up, showing up, and staying up all day*. Sometimes when in a mind-body rebuild or reboot, starting with "I love you, body" can be enough. Other times, we may need to whip out the big guns of accountability, appreciation, and humility.

Guidance Can Help

Another big gun to consider is seeking out the assistance of a guide, coach or therapist, depending on your flavor of support you desire. This can be a lot like going to the gym. It doesn't take much to show up and start lifting some weights randomly. However, if you desire to achieve a specific goal, it's often more efficient to get the help of a professional trainer to guide you in your pursuit, and even motivate you along the way. I view my collaborations with my clients in similar terms. I, too, reach out for assistance when I feel blocked in my personal pain releases, and life's transitions and transformations.

Practice Makes Progress

Keep in mind: performing this forgiveness meditation once will not be enough to remedy chronic pain, especially at first. Once is not going to recover a lifetime of neglect, or even worse, abuse of your body. If you've consumed only fast food and soda for ten years, ten days in the gym is not going to "fix" that.

The cool thing, however, about starting this practice is giving your body the chance to be heard by you. If you have been ignoring its truths for decades, it may not completely trust you at first. Each day you choose to do a loving check-in, it helps to remind the body that you do care and you are present. Even the short version of the forgiveness meditation can make a world of difference in honoring and deepening the mind-body-soul connection:

I hear you. I see you. I feel you. I love you uncond-itionally and accept you fully. How can I support you?

Any little bit of movement towards our peace, balance and pain-free living is a movement to positivity and in the direction we want to go. If you don't go from a nine to a zero, that's okay— be forgiving! Forgive your body for not being willing or able to move the way you need. Forgive yourself for taking so long to listen to your body's messages. Remember the young child tugging a parent's sleeve? That's your body. How do you respond? Would you answer her or him with aggression, disregard or punishment? Of course not.

If you have spent a lifetime treating your body like a machine, ignoring its pleas and warnings, it can become resentful. While forgiveness, consideration, and love can reverse that animosity, it takes patience and time—longer for some than others. So, begin your forgiveness meditation practice and be grateful for any feeling of progress you make. Be patient with yourself and remember the tortoise won the race.

Learn how to trust yourself again and let the body know that it's alright that it doesn't trust you. If you have ever been in an abusive relationship of any kind (verbally, mentally or physically), you may be familiar with this classic response

Just because you learned something from your parents or society does not mean it is correct or the only way to do something. Don't be afraid to step out of the box and try something different. Even if things don't turn out exactly as planned, acting in alignment with your truth builds confidence. You will find that your fears automatically fall away as you realize you had nothing to fear in the first place. It is liberating!

Are you staying true to yourself?

Don't let the fear of being judged by someone change what you do or who you become. Be your authentic self and the best version of you that you can be!

Without a doubt, one of the greatest things I've learned is how to manifest what I want; it has helped me grow my business and draw other wonderful things into my life. I have also been able to help some of my clients shift their energy and thoughts as well. The law of attraction works. If our focus is on fear or judgment (even subconsciously), that is what we bring into our lives. For example, if we are focused on not wanting to be in horrible relationships, we are going to keep attracting them. We need to shift our focus to what kind of relationship we do want, not the kind we don't!

A few years ago, I decided I wanted to build a healing room on the side of my house so that I would have a sacred space to see clients. When I first started talking with my husband about building a room, I had all of these amazing pictures in my head of what I wanted it to look like. I became excited as we discussed ideas about how to make it happen. Then came all the reasons why we should not build it—too much money, no room, not enough time, it wouldn't be worth it—and I would lose hope of it ever becoming a reality. A few months later, the subject would come up again and the same thing would happen. I felt like I was on a rollercoaster ride, and eventually, I gave up. Then someone told me to start visualizing the room as if I already had it. I stopped talking to my husband about it and started seeing it in my mind. I saw the wood on the walls, the flooring, how it was decorated and what the windows looked like. I pictured it every night before I went to bed and I dreamed about it constantly. I even found myself buying things to put in it. I accumulated a great pile of items in the corner of a spare bedroom in our house. I started journaling things like, "I am so grateful for my beautiful room, and I love it! The energy in it feels amazing!" Then I started to visualize seeing clients in it and journaling about that as well. I was writing things like, "I saw six clients today, and their experience was incredible and so much healing occurred," and "I taught a Reiki class to ten students yesterday and it was amazing," and so on.

One day I came home from work and found my husband's cousin there visiting. Imagine my shock when he said to me, "Let's go out and see where you want your windows and doors." What? I had not even mentioned the room to my husband in months! His cousin and I made some plans, and he told me he would be back at the end of March. My room was finished that May, and by mid-June, I was seeing clients in it. I taught my first class in there in the middle of August. Once I let go of my expectations and the outcome, I manifested that room into my physical reality! I had to put my thoughts out there and trust that it would be built, and it was.

You and your clients can use the same type of practice to manifest what you want:

1. Let go of the need and expectation to know exactly how you are going to get it, or when. Establish a loose timeframe: six months, one year, so that you are putting the feeling of it out there.

2. Visualize it like you have it already. I mean really see it.

3. Feel it, taste it, hear it, breathe it.

4. Live it, talk about it constantly.

5. Journal about it consistently.

6. Keep all thoughts about it positive, and never give up!

There you have it, some of the simplest yet most powerful tools and exercises I've learned along my journey. They have had a huge impact on my life, and I hope they do the same for you.

To recap, get a planner and get organized. Start a daily routine: meditation, listening to music, journaling, taking care of you. Start your practice of gratitude. Don't worry what others think, and embrace your fears. Don't be afraid to think outside of the box and step out of your comfort zone. Surround yourself with a great support system and use it. Be kind, compassionate, gentle, loving and forgiving with yourself. Stay true to who you are! And always remember, you are loved, you are enough, you matter and you've got this!

As I like to say, "Never let fear stand in between saddling up to follow your dreams!"

CHAPTER

Thirteen

Healer's Cocoon
by Jeannie Church

JEANNIE CHURCH

Jeannie Church is a Divorce Mediator, Coach and Healer. Her passion is changing how couples experience divorce by advocating for resilience and peace during the process. With a Master of Somatic Psychology, she has a holistic approach for compassionately working with the stress and trauma that separation can impose on the mind, body, soul and spirit. Jeannie is also a Reiki Level II practitioner, a Gong Goddess and nature-lover. When she is not mediating, you may find her playing with crystals or somewhere on a shamanic journey.

https://www.truedirectiondivorce.com/
https://birdbrown.com/
jeannie.m.church@gmail.com
720.722.4159

Acknowledgments

I have been blessed with so many bright healers who have gracefully, and with impeccable timing, invited me onto my healing paths and held a lantern of light while I stumbled around in the dark. They have offered pure friendship and support beyond comprehension. They are love. I give my gratitude to each of you (and many more) for being with me from beginning to who knows when. In alphabetical order by first name, they are:

Ashley Owen, Autumn Starr, Church family, Dana Spirit Butterfly, Dani Bartov, Deborah Bryant, Dina Faye Gilmore, former husbands, Gretchen Stecher, Jason Dombrow, Jeannie Sajonas, Jeannette Acosta/Sat Siri Kaur, Kyra Schaefer, Landmark Worldwide, Lois and John Church, Meaghan Miller Lopez, Naropa University-Somatic Psych Graduate Program, Richard Booth, Robert Niles, Shannon Brennan, Yogi Bhajan, Yolanda Dandridge.

Healer's Cocoon
By Jeannie Church

We have all heard the story of the butterfly breaking out of its cocoon and flying free. In that story, the freedom associated with breaking out is what we tend to focus on. Instead, what if we focus on the time the butterfly spends *in* the cocoon?

I believe in the power of the cocoon. We all know that it's a place where transformation happens, hence, the butterfly. The question is how does that transformation take place? What does the caterpillar go through to become the butterfly? What do you go through to become a healer?

During metamorphosis, it's messy in the cocoon. The caterpillar digests itself and most of it is original, recognizable traits turn into soup. Then, the new cells split and multiply to begin forming the butterfly. During this time, it is important that the cocoon remains undisturbed so that the process can be completed.

In nature, chances are that the cocooning caterpillar will be disturbed or devoured by a bird. The same goes for us, but we likely won't be devoured by a bird! When we engage in an intentional healing process, the time in the healing cocoon will likely be interrupted or feel like it has been cut short. There's even the feeling that it's taking too long to experience your butterfly-self. Our healing can be disrupted by life events: marriage, family, children, divorce, illness and death. All of life can rush in and smother the precious time we are trying to take to heal ourselves and mend our wounds. At this point, it should be apparent that the use of a cocoon is a metaphor for having an intentional, undisturbed space and time in which to heal your wounds, get to know yourself on a deeper level and, in some way, transform.

Throughout my life, I have spent time in and out of various metaphorical cocoons. The amount of *time* spent in the cocoon matters less than *why* and *how* I spent that time in the cocoon. I have been consciously and unwittingly healing myself on a soul level for about 16 of my 50 years, and in lifetimes longer. I have often berated myself for how long it has taken me to get exactly where I am. I have frequently referred to myself as a late bloomer. After much soulful and spiritual work, I am happy to say, my timing for breaking free and spreading my wings is perfect. Your timing is also perfect.

If my timing is now perfect, why would I choose to spend any time intentionally cocooning? First, I would do it to heal and learn to love me. Then, I would discover and experience my ultimate purpose. Go existentially big or go home! It turns out that my ultimate purpose includes inspiring healing for others, and the big picture is (drumroll please) raising the potential healing vibration of our planet. Does this make me a healer? I've been told that it does, and that I am a healer.

I am a healer that did not overtly inherit any special healing gifts from my family. I did not have obvious psychic or mediumship abilities (until recently). I did not recognize myself as such because the healer in me works in subtle ways. The healer in me has been hiding and, one could even say, cocooning. As I trained, developed and learned, I reached a metamorphic tipping point, and now must share what I know and the special gifts I discovered along the way.

People on this planet need healing. Being a divorce mediator, I meet and speak with people every day who need healing. I have been married and divorced three times. It has become clear that my soul's plan in this life included major challenges with love, commitment and marriage. I have been exploring and healing my body, soul and spirit through this lens of divorce. As I have shared my journey with people throughout the years, I heal, and in some resonant ways, so do they.

Whether I was the one leaving or vice versa, each time divorce happened, it was like a shock wave hit my life. Everything would shatter and then numbness would set in. Negotiations and begging would ensue. It has brought me to the lowest places and the lowest vibrations. It reduced my self-esteem to minuscule levels and added to an already high level of shame. My first instinct then was to hide, so I did. I let everything fall away from me save a few lifeline friendships.

I have come to understand that I am here to experience deep healing, love, joy and the freedom to fully be myself. Before reaching this glorious place of deep love and understanding, it took intention, vulnerability and time. Some of which, I spent in an intentional healing cocoon.

There is a distinct difference between hiding and cocooning oneself. Hiding is mainly motivated by unconscious fear and shame. I believe healing can happen because a person seeks it, initiates it or it spontaneously arises. Cocooning is motivated by an intentional, conscious desire to understand you and offer yourself deeply felt compassion. I now see that compassion (not fear) is the key to deep self-understanding and self-acceptance. You may find that hiding your healing gifts zaps you of energy which would be better spent in more appropriate ways. I encourage you to spend time intentionally cocooning with imagination and intuition and less time hiding.

Unless you're someone who is already in touch with your healer-self, look to see if a healer is hiding dormant within you. Imagine for a few moments that, on a basic level, we come into each other's lives to naturally heal each other no matter what the exchange. Every encounter could be an opportunity for healing. What if you are a healer and maybe you forgot? I imagine that every person I come into contact with offers an opportunity to heal myself or them to be healed by me.

All interactions are energetic vibrations which can cause growth, healing and integration on a soul level and personality level. Sometimes, I am the healer because others are inspired by my ability to heal myself which, in turn, invites people to find the courage to begin their healing paths.

Early on, my cocoon took many forms. It began with Kundalini Yoga and Teacher's Training. I continued by getting a Masters in Somatic Psychology. It also took the form of an in-depth psychotherapeutic process for me. It was years of personal growth and development programs. My most recent healing comes by way of shamanic journeying, psychic channeling, deeply exploring past lives, intuitive crystal and sound healing sessions and lots of nature.

Exploring and discovering your healing process is unique to you. My exploration has been an amalgamation of the wisdom I have heard, read, been taught directly or spontaneously experienced. While I chose the path of least resistance with almost all my chosen modalities, there was an exception, and that was my Masters in Somatic Psychology. During those three years of intense cocooning, my personality was deconstructed, much like the caterpillar digesting itself into some cellular soup. The process exposed mostly shadows so I could heal those hidden parts of me. That's not the path for everyone. As a healer, the tools I have resonated most with me have remained in my wheelhouse. The beauty of them is that one dovetails into the next one, and they conjure a particular movement and soulful prose that wants to be seen, heard and, ultimately, healed.

Each one of those modalities offers a profound heart-aching, soul-splitting process to truly heal yourself on all levels. It's not always fluffy and nice in that cocoon. You are essentially disrupting the current reality you hold. Breaking your reality is not to be taken lightly—it offers an untethered quality to life that can be difficult for your ego and personality to reconcile. At some point, the desire to heal becomes stronger than the pattern of remaining in your habitual suffering of mind and body. A cocoon created intentionally by you and for you is a beautiful way to nurture yourself back to wholeness and perhaps coax the healer in you to come out and play.

In everything I studied, I did so because there was a great desire to deepen the experience. The desire to heal myself always came first. This is not the case with every healer. Some receive a calling or a direct message early on and are compelled to answer that call. It was not that way for me. My path has been a slow burn. I had been feeling shameful about not being as certain or as pure as other healers. This was nonsense. At least, it makes no sense now that I am fully embracing my unique way of healing.

If you are struggling with who you are as a healer, drop in and deepen your experience of healing yourself. If you experience self-doubt, I invite you to dive deeper in search of you—not others—you. Your soul is only interested in you.

A healing process can conjure emotion and vulnerability like no other. It can bring you to your knees and raise you up high. It can offer waves of movement and release that have a desire to cycle through fully. The shortest path is to follow the energy and trust it to take you where you need to be. If the energy seems inappropriate for you, bring curiosity and question it; redirect it. You can become the master of your healing energy.

"What the caterpillar calls the end of the world, the master calls a butterfly." —Richard Bach

Here are some compassionate ways I explore myself, my soul and the healer in me. Please use it to understand and love yourself at every moment. Use it as a loose framework for exploration and spontaneously change it, following your unique flow.

Tips:

1. Don't be afraid to get messy in the cocoon. That's a big part of why you would create it. This is a time to let go, shed old ways and patterns, then begin the

work of splitting cells and forming new ones, transforming and getting closer to your original meant-to-be self or oneness with your soul. The more I understand my soul holds us with total compassion, the more of a healer I become.

2. Whatever shows up inside this precious time, you get to choose how to interpret it and what to do with it. I encourage you to feel whatever shows up without judgment. Increase your level of curiosity about yourself, your body and your soul. This is such good practice for self-love and compassion.

3. This could also be time for romancing yourself and the healer in you. The cocoon doesn't always need to get messy, and you can hold the intention of pure love and romance.

4. Trust yourself and follow your impulse for how to spend time in your cocoon.

Prompts:

Here are some prompts for you to contemplate inside and outside of your cocoon:

- Show me the healer in me.
- Show me how to deepen my experience of loving myself.
- Show me my way.
- How do I already naturally heal others I come into contact with?

- What gifts are hidden from me and ready to reveal themselves?

- What is my way?

Cocooning Meditation:

1. You are about to create a beautiful cocoon to hold all of you and open a dialogue with your life.

2. Set aside a minimum of one hour. Two hours is wonderful; the whole day is divine or longer.

3. Gather sheepskins, soft blankets, meditation pillows and maybe wrap yourself in your favorite shawl.

4. Smudge the space with smoke and prayers.

5. Give yourself permission to talk with all of your soul and personality and surround yourself with your sacred objects. Walk around your cocoon; touch crystals, objects and books that are potent and precious to you. Greet them and thank them for their beauty. As you are called to, bring objects to the cocoon nest you built. Continue to weave your cocoon.

6. Light a candle, a couple or a few.

7. Have water or tea close by.

8. Lay your journal within arm's reach.

9. Can you visualize it? This is your cocoon.

10. Be with your body. You've done it a thousand times, but do it inside this cocoon. Notice your breath and continue by sending breath, love and light, beginning

with your toes and following the natural drift of energy.

11. Greet your body much the same way you greeted the objects and space when you began with gratitude, compassion and love for its beauty and strength to carry you through.

12. You might feel the impulse to place your arms around yourself (yes, hold yourself) and rock yourself.

13. You might feel the impulse to focus on your third eye and tune in with your intuitive self and follow colors and images that appear.

14. Be here in this soft cocooning space for as long as you have or need to. If you are dealing with a recent trauma and feel you want extra support, have your closest resource on speed dial or wait until you sense your readiness to be totally alone with yourself.

15. Exiting the cocoon is as soft as entering. Give gratitude for all that transpired and thank your body and soul and perhaps say, "See you again soon, my loves."

In the beginning of this chapter, I asked the question, "What do you go through to become a healer?" I offer you the answer that you go through "everything." Everything you experience, everything you heal, every part of yourself you bring home and nurture and let go, it all conjures the healer in you. Through cocooning, I hope you too can find your way out of the darkness of yourself as your healer.

A poem for the road:

Here she comes

Welcome sister in the dark

Lurk in the shadows no more

I open my arms to you and say, come play in this cocoon

There is light and love here

Let us be embraced and commune here with our soul

CHAPTER

Fourteen

Harmony By Karate Method
by John Mirrione

JOHN MIRRIONE

Sensei John P. Mirrione has been training in karate for 40 years. He was bullied severely, and this led to him being a lifelong teacher who focuses on the healing aspects of the martial arts. He is the founder of Harmony By Karate that is rated in the top 10 martial arts schools in the U.S.

Sensei John took his martial arts expertise and combined it with breakdancing, leading to him becoming a well-known solo dance performer. As an Air Force entertainer, he danced all over the country. This later led him to having four performances at the Apollo Theater, and 72 episodes of Club MTV which broadened his understanding of human equality and celebrating diversity through dance.

He traveled to 17 cities to get a glimpse into the bullying crisis in the U.S. This deepened his understanding of the root causes of bullying. As a result, he founded the Harmony Power Foundation. Its mission is to "stand up to bullying and stand for human equality." He was a featured guest on Deepak Chopra's One World, discussing the healing aspects of empowering children on a worldwide scale.

Most recently, Sensei John set a new world record, doing 42 one-arm/one-leg push-ups in 30 seconds to teach children that anything is possible when you put your mind and great consistent effort into it.

His experience as a martial artist and dancer led to him living a more fearless existence as he achieved countless goals. His main goal is guiding the planet to heal itself is by empowering humanity to look deep inside and make the necessary changes to make the world a safer, happier, and healthier place to live and thrive.

Acknowledgments

To my friends, family, and most importantly, our divine guidance. My divine guidance is Jesus, the archangels, and all highest spirit beings of all time.

Harmony By Karate Method
By John P Mirrione

Presence Heals

"Now is the future of yesterday and the past of tomorrow."
—Sensei John

When we think of presence, we think of being grounded, rooted in the earth, and centered in who we are. When we're centered, we can learn focus, discipline, and respect, affording us the chance to experience personal transformation as well as physical agility. Like a turtle that moves slowly and spends much of its long life in stillness, when we focus on being in the now, we lose the sense of time and become timeless. A practice as simple as deep breathing can do wonders for our ability to learn presence, such as the position of child's pose in yoga. This feeling of deep presence will bring joy in our day to day life. As we continue to cultivate this concept, we are learning to deeply listen to our inner selves, raising our inner vibration and intuitive consciousness.

Once we have this great presence with ourselves, we can apply it to our relationships. We can spend more time deeply listening to our lovers, friends, and family. Either our relationships will greatly deepen or we will awaken to the idea that some of these relationships no longer serve us. Most importantly, bringing a deeper presence in ourselves will transcend our relationships and bring great joy and fulfillment. Everything we do and everything we are is all about connecting to others in meaningful ways.

Openness Heals

Once we become present, we can open our minds and hearts more to teachings. With an open heart and mind, we learn tolerance. From tolerance emerges an acceptance of who we are. This acceptance expands to include others, deepening our connection to humanity.

Choosing to be open to how we feel inside and then being open to making the changes we intuitively know we need to make to transform and evolve our soul is why we are here together on this planet.

When I was 40 years old, I developed a life-threatening case of pneumonia. I spent eight days in the hospital. While in the hospital, I spoke to one of the mentors, who later became a dear friend, martial arts icon, Leo Fong. He told me that the only way to recover was through deep breathing. I then began conscious, slow, deep breathing. I recovered so strongly that my lungs felt stronger than before the pneumonia. Breathing practice has become an integral part of my life, and deep breathing is integrated into all training sessions at Harmony By Karate. My choice of being open in mind and in my breath was essential to survival. This open-mindedness to learn saved my life, and two years later, I was able to swim the full length of a swimming pool without coming up for air!

Giving Heals

It's important for us to be giving, both in our movements and in every aspect of our lives. In martial arts, when someone is attacking, the student gives way, exactly like water yields around an object. Then, the student closes back around the attacker. The attack can be physical or emotional. Water is an extremely powerful element, and when we practice movements that flow like the water that we are, it raises our energetic vibration, improves our vitality, and brings great power to our overall being. Applying the idea of giving physical movement into spiritual interaction is truly a profound experience when we choose.

The most important thing you can give to anyone is your time. Time can never be taken back. When we give our time and do it with love, what we give to the other is already given back. The act of giving feels amazing, and there is no longer a need to have an expectation of a return. Living life in such a way that we give love in all of our interactions is incredibly powerful and transformative.

Courage Heals

Courage is the one quality that is required for our transformation. In order to change, we must have enough courage to face our fear. Developing courage is a three-step process. The first step is to face the fear: to see it, look at it, and acknowledge it. The second step is to embrace the fear, to accept it, and acknowledge that it's real. The third step is to conquer the fear either by taking a small step or a bounding leap. In martial arts, if a student is sparring with another student who seems bigger, the student must first experience this massive force. Then, acknowledging and accepting the anxiety is crucial. Finally, their next choice is to conquer it. This can be done by one small step, such as a punch, kick, or a bounding leap, using several hand or foot techniques in one burst.

I remember being at a tournament many years ago and confronting an opponent who was seemingly impossible to beat. He was about 6' 7" and 250 pounds to my 5' 6" and 140 pounds at that time. He was destroying me until I realized it was not about competition. He had evil in his eyes, and kicked me so hard I became airborne, landing onto the spectators and bleachers. I was kicked in the groin and punched in the face until I woke up. I knew I needed to break his spirit to survive. After I charged him with a leg kick and a flurry of punches, the match quickly came into my favor. After several matches of me chasing this seemingly impossible warrior to beat, I realized that anything is possible. It takes great courage to stand up to your greatest fears. This will liberate and heal your soul. Anyone can physically harm another, but if you stand up verbally and physically, your spirit prevails!

Harmony Heals

Harmony is the ability to balance all things. When we're present, we can be open. When we're open, we can give. Giving is the most courageous act, and inspires more courage. When we're present, open and give with courage, we can source balance and harmony within ourselves and in our world. When we achieve this, there is only a deepening of peace and self-belief in what we do. Peace and harmony are not destinations; they are journeys. Harmony is discovered and deepened only through dealing with our challenges with relationships, particularly, the relationships within ourselves. Spirit represents our life energy, and the butterfly embodies harmony. It flies, lands, and interacts with other beings as a harmonious, beautiful, flowing, free being. It has enough courage to land fearlessly on a much bigger creature, such as a human. The way of the butterfly is gentle.

Power Heals

Our inner power is the life force in us that defines who we are. It is our energy field, aura, spirit, soul, and inner vibration. Here, we discover our power of creativity. This creative source must be challenged to evolve our soul. This creative aspect of our being defines our life purpose. Using this purpose is our gift to serve all humanity in all ways possible.

Our thoughts dictate all of our experiences. What we think all the time truly impacts how we feel and all the relationships we attract. Science has already proven that our thoughts directly impact our DNA on a physical level. Therefore, if we think we are strong, flexible and smart, it will significantly impact how we feel physically and mentally.

If we think we can't do it, it is likely we never will. If we think we can, we most likely will. To affirm is to say, "I can do anything." This idea said throughout the day will impact how we feel, what we do, and what we will attract each and every moment. When we are met with great adversity, it is the best time to say, "I can do it!"

Freedom Heals

Freedom is spontaneous and unpredictable. We are free and only constrained by our imagination and ability.

Whenever we have fear to conquer our goal or plan, we must choose to conquer this fear to liberate our soul. This is a never-ending concept. As we meditate/pray and take action on these fears, your spirit becomes more liberated. The joy it brings is immeasurable. Avoid those voices, whether they are yours or others', who say that you can't, and know all things are possible and you can affect things in your life you never thought possible.

CHAPTER

Fifteen

Sarang "Love" Method
by Dr. Juju Love

DR. JUJU LOVE

Dr. YoungJu Lee (a.k.a. Dr. JuJu Love) is a transformative holistic wellness goddess. Prior to her career in the
wellness industry, she served as an art director in New York
City for over a decade. When the company was acquired by
a consumer market giant, she took the opportunity to walk
away and pursue her quest for self-discovery in full force.
During her journey, she experienced a spiritual awakening
that transformed her life into that of a healer in service to

humanity. She's been walking the path of a healer for the past 15 years. Along her journey, she became a licensed naturopathic doctor in the state of Arizona. Her passion is to guide people to their soul/spiritual awakening so they can live the life they are meant to with love, peace, joy and harmony. Visit her at www.SarangMethod.com

Acknowledgments

My heartfelt thanks and deepest appreciation goes to my friends, family, my inner goddess and the divine guidance from the *source* and beings of *divine love and light*.

Sarang "Love" Method
by Dr. JuJu Love

Sarang means "love" in Korean. Love heals.

The Gift

You are a gift from the divine to yourself and to the world.

Have you ever marveled at what an incredibly magical miracle you are? Think for a moment. Out of this vast universe of countless galaxies, stars and planets, you happened to be experiencing life right here on Earth at this particular time in history. Not only that, do you know the odds of your being conceived as you? It's far beyond one in a million. At the time of your conception, there was an epic race where one winner took all. So, millions upon millions of your dad's little warrior princes, sperm, jumped out gleefully and dove right into your mom's vagina in a state of nothing short of bliss. Luckily for the little princes, everything was in a perfect condition that particular day for the race to the goddess. So, they began their journey of life and death. Sadly, most didn't make it to the end, and only a fraction of them got to see the luminous glorious goddess, the egg, on the outside. Here, each little fierce warrior prince gave his best attempt at his last feat in getting through to the goddess. Finally, the best of the best got in and the gate to the goddess was shut to all the other remaining little princes. When the goddess and the winning warrior prince merged as one, there was a spark of life which

174

then divided and grew and eventually came out into this world as you.

Can you now grasp what went into creating you? You have within you the ultimate winning spirit, tenacity, courage, strength, focus and determination of a warrior prince who won against 40-200 million others! The reason why I'm telling you this story is because so many of you tend to forget what took place in creating you and what an absolute miracle you are. The conception story is only a small portion of who you are because you are also a part of a divine being, and one can't even begin to fathom what might have taken place in you in the spirit realm.

The universe orchestrated your birth and delivered you because you truly are a gift to the world. This gift wants to be expressed and needs to be shared with the world, and the only one who can do that is you. You hold power to this gift and the key to unlock it, and if you're reading this book, it is no mistake that the time has come for you to boldly step into your light and shine your light by sharing the gift that you are.

It All Begins with Love

There's a rainbow in each and every one of you. All you look for in life will be found when you look within.

Have you ever stopped and pondered the meaning of *love*? From my personal experience, there's only *love*, the *oneness*, all that is, and we are all part of it. We feel joy when we flow in this soup of love. However, our brilliant human minds often play tricks on us that give us an illusion of being separate from all that is, and the illusion of separation is what brings about different shades of negative emotions we experience: sadness, anger, frustration, hate, rage and blame.

This love is all encompassing. It is all there is and all that you are. When you embrace this love in your heart, the world becomes that love, peace and harmony. In order to find this love in your heart, you need to first understand what is going on inside of you.

As you torment yourself emotionally, you torment your body physically as well. People talk about the wars going on in the world, but we need to find peace within us before we can heal the world from wars. There are wars going on inside of your body all the time. Some of your body parts, organs and systems have forgotten how to communicate properly with one another, leaving you with pains, illnesses and diseases.

Once you mentally, emotionally and physically find peace and balance in yourself, you will be able to find peace within and better connect with your spirit. You will start to realize who you are as a spirit being. You underestimate the grandness you possess. If you can open your inner eyes even a little, you will begin to see the world in a whole new way; you will begin to see light in places where all you saw was darkness in the past. When you begin to operate from your heart with love, you will realize that love truly heals everything and everyone around you, even when things seem to be completely out of balance and order. Love brings light to illuminate and transform darkness, hate, despair, sadness and everything you associate as the negative experience into that of love.

What is true alchemy? It is love. When love transmutes hate and fear into love, this is true alchemy. We are all alchemists. You have the power within you to transmute and transform what you call darkness and negativity into love and light. You are love and light, the carrier of the divine essence. The more you exercise the divine alchemical powers, the stronger and brighter you become. It all begins within you. When you begin to love yourself, forgive yourself and allow your love and light to grow and glow within and without you, you will be able to transform everything around you in the same love and light.

In order to recognize your love and light, it would take courage to be truly vulnerable enough to surrender to your weaknesses. You then learn to allow yourself to accept and receive love and support that can guide you to transform the weaknesses by propelling you through a springboard of experiences to an empowered self. It is the evolution of you becoming the embodiment of divine love and light that would light up all your chakras, the energy vortexes, in all colors of the rainbow.

Mind

Energy flows where the mind goes. Being aware of your mental processes and states is the beginning of healing.

Your thoughts, emotions and physical illnesses are intricately connected. Negative thoughts create negative emotions, attributing to stress. There are different types of stresses, but often it's the invisible emotional stresses that have a huge impact on the state of your wellbeing, and you can affect them by shifting your mindset about them.

When you have a thought, your brain reacts by producing neurochemicals that start a cascade of biochemical and physiological changes. They trigger certain emotions that affect your hormones. Hormones are like little messengers that affect all the cells in your body. Over time, if you are prone to think in a certain negative way about something, your body will keep producing the same neurochemicals, making you feel the same emotions and affecting your whole physiology. Over time, this creates your habits, addictions and even physical diseases.

Whatever you think about, you feed it to grow and manifest in your life. It is important to pay attention and cultivate a positive mindset about your thought processes through a regular practice. Spend at least a few minutes a day sitting quietly and observing your thoughts without judging, and practice letting thoughts float away. Add some deep breathing to this practice, and in no time, you will start noticing some positive effects such as relaxation and less anxiety.

Body

The body has the innate intelligence to heal itself. In order for it to do its job properly, the obstacles to healing need to be removed. Then, the right resources for healing and restoration need to be given.

You are a conscious being and your body has consciousness. Every cell and every part of your body has its unique consciousness. It knows what its purpose is and what it needs to do. For example, if you get a cut, different parts of your body will work together to heal the wound. Your blood coagulates and stops bleeding. There may be some immune cells involved so it doesn't get infected and your skin matrix starts to mend the cut. At any given moment, your body diligently conducts a fine orchestra of multiple systems, organs and trillions of cells to work together in harmony. However, today's medicine tends to approach the body as if it's a machine that falls short when it comes to healing the whole person. The human body is not like a machine that can be repaired by replacing broken parts. Every part of the body is connected to the whole body/mind/spirit system and they work together. You cannot separate the heart from the brain or the brain from the gut. Every part of the body is interconnected to the whole, and if one part suffers, the whole body will be affected.

If there are hindrances to the healing of the body, whether they are physical, mental or emotional, they need to be removed. The body also requires the proper nutrients needed to nurture and nourish it. Food is the best medicine. Mindfully choosing foods that nourish and heal your body and eating the foods with love and gratitude will help your body heal in a way you didn't even know possible.

Spirit

We are spirits having human experiences.

When you connect with that higher aspect of yourself, everything you experience in life will be divinely guided for your highest good and the highest good of all. It takes dedication and effort to create a harmonious connection between the mind, body and spirit. Some of the best practices my clients and I benefit from are a combination of regular meditation, journaling and some form of physical activities such as exercises, yoga, Tai Chi, Qi Gong, breathing exercises and even dancing.

The spiritual development of a human parallels that of the physical development. Similar to a child being born, then growing up to be an adult by going through the adolescence, coming of age, to becoming his or her person, so is the spiritual development. When I experienced my spiritual awakening 15 years ago, it felt like I was a spirit child with newfound toys, followed by years of learning, practicing, owning and embodying my gifts and skills. I now recognize that I have all the tools and skills to stand on my own as a goddess of love still evolving. I am proud and I feel free to be seen as who I am, a fully-fledged goddess of love and light in all her glory, soaring into the heights she's never flown before, and radiating her brilliance brighter than ever before. With this awareness and experience of freedom to be who I am, I find it important and pertinent to discuss "coming out of the closet" because this is how you can boldly step into your light, radiating your light and sharing the gift that you are.

Coming Out of the Closet as a Spirit Being

What is freedom and what does it feel like to be free to be who you truly are?

Coming out of the closet," means coming out of hiding. I believe it's time that humans go beyond the LGBT community with this movement because accepting who you are and allowing yourself to be seen as your authentic self needs to be exercised by all. I am grateful that the LGBT community has paved the way to make it accessible for the rest of us. They have already done their soul searching to realize it's better to risk losing everything outside of them than losing who they are. Even if it means losing their family, friends, jobs and being ostracized, the ultimate gain is the freedom. If your blood relatives and friends abandon you, you can build a new family with those who truly love, support and accept you for who you are.

How many of you can truly say you have embraced who you are and are living an authentic life? If you are still in the closet waiting for the perfect moment where you feel safe to come out, I invite you to explore the following self-inquiry exercises to guide you to your freedom and power so that you can radiate and share your love and light with the world the way you are meant to.

6 Self-Inquiry Exercises

Gift yourself with a dedicated time to journal about these exercises. First, ask the question and thank God, creator, your higher self or whomever you share your spiritual connection with by acknowledging that you have already received the answer. Then, close your eyes and listen quietly to your heart's whisper, and start writing down whatever comes to your mind without hesitating, censoring or judging. Let it flow and trust in the process.

1. **"Who am I?"**
   The inner and outer transformation will begin with this simple philosophical question. You have been conditioned to identify yourself with titles, labels and expectations that have been placed upon you by family, friends, culture, society and even yourself.
2. **What is your passion and purpose in life?**

Ask yourself what makes your heart sing with joy, what gets you out of bed and what makes you feel alive. Recall your childhood aspirations. As a child, you were deeply connected to your soul and you knew who you were intrinsically. Connecting to that essence can be a great clue to the answer you're searching for.

3. **Why is it important for you to come out of the closet now?**
   Go into your heart-space and explore what the benefits are for you to "come out" now. What do you gain from opening that door and coming out into the world as who you are now? Does the timing matter?

4. **What would be the consequence of you not coming out of the closet?**
   Explore what would happen if you remained in the closet, the risks of staying in the dark and not being able to shine your light and share your gift. How do you feel about that?

5. **What is your biggest fear about coming out of the closet?**
   Be honest with yourself and identify your fears, however big or small, regarding the act of coming out of the closet and revealing your truth to the world. Where do your fears come from and how have they been affecting your life?

6. **What is one thing you can do today that will bring you one step closer to opening that closet door and stepping out of it?**
   Tune into the small action steps you can take towards your freedom to being your authentic self. Are you willing to take the steps? If you fall, will you get up again?

CHAPTER

Sixteen

A Healing Journey
With Sound
by Kat Saraswati

KAT SARASWATI

Kat Saraswati, the founder of Serenity Through Sound®, is best known for her work in harmonic and sound therapy. Raised in a verbally and physically abusive environment, she developed a belief of being unworthy of love and happiness. She abused her body and allowed others to do the same which fueled self-disgust and self-hate. It was through the unwavering and unconditional love of her husband that she found the courage to heal the relationship with herself and others. She is devoted to inspiring individuals to overcome perceived limitations and challenges by developing the courage to re-evaluate their judgments, projections, points of view and behaviors.

Kat earned a bachelor's degree in computer science with an emphasis in software engineering, a master's degree in systems engineering, and has achieved multiple sound and harmonic therapy certifications. She has a successful career with the federal government as a senior program manager. Kat rejoices in life without boundaries or definition—a continuous generative state of being—fueling her soul and inspiring her to facilitate the healing of others and the environment.

Serenity Through Sound®
www.SerenityThroughSound.com
717.516.1164 contact@SerenityThroughSound.com

Acknowledgments

Dean R. Baker, Erin Shrader, Meredith Kaminek, Ann L. Smull, Cynthia Stromvall, Kara Shiffer, Francis G. Demain, Frances M. Edmonds, Paulene Goodman, Mitch Nur, Ph.D., Don Conreaux, Taunya Rivera, Sista Connie, Betsy Ingram, Nataleah Rose Schotte, Jonathan Schotte, Tok Tamang, Craig Shankster, Aimee Zimmerman, Janet Young, Cathy Brown.

A Healing Journey with Sound
by Kat Saraswati

For over 30 years, I searched for ways to overcome the physical and mental traumas of my childhood and abusive relationships during my teen and young adult life. I sought treatment with psychologists, psychiatrists, shamans, Reiki practitioners, and metaphysical healers. It was not until I was gifted a massage therapy session that integrated Himalayan singing bowls that a major shift in my mental and physical state occurred. The vibration penetrated me deeply and opened an awareness within me. I knew the vibrational energy of the singing bowls would become an integral part of my healing journey. To educate myself, I researched Himalayan singing bowls, practitioners and sound healing. I spent years working with world-renowned Master Teacher, Mitch Nur, Ph.D., learning playing techniques, tuning my listening skills and learning cultural philosophy. As my knowledge and skills increased, I developed a strong passion for educating others on the therapeutic benefits of harmonics, sound, and vibration.

However, I questioned my abilities and pondered if having a strong desire to share the gift of sound was sufficient. I could feel my mind and body becoming overwhelmed with self-doubt and fear. The more I dwelled on my perceived weaknesses, the greater resistance I created to realizing my potential. How would it be when I did not have my teacher, mentors, and peers around to support me? What would I do or how would I react if the client did not receive the session the way I expected? It was not until I performed my first session without the physical support of my teacher, mentors, and peers that I embraced my gift. I had an epiphany that the magic happens when fully in the allowance of everything and anything. I hope to inspire you to pursue the gift that you are and realize the infinite contribution you bring to this world.

What is sound healing therapy?

The modality of sound, harmonics, and vibration has multiple paths and serves many purposes. Using sound tools for personal healing can create greater awareness and expansion of one's consciousness. The sound and vibration of these sacred tools penetrate your being and tap into emotions embodied in the cellular fibers of the body. This modality has a plethora of avenues of study and instruments that can be quite overwhelming for a newcomer. One of the big misconceptions is the requirement to have a musical background, prior experience playing an instrument or be musically inclined—this is not true. You may encounter many sound healers and therapists who are trained musicians, singers, or composers or have some musical background. However, most are music therapists and not necessarily sound therapists. Music therapy and sound therapy share similar principles, yet have significantly different techniques and applications. Trust in the knowledge and allow yourself to learn along the way.

Begin the Journey

Where and how to start? What equipment and training are required? Begin the journey and exploration of sound, harmonics and vibrational healing by asking:

- What about sound, harmonics, and vibration resonates within me and my body?
- Which sound tools bring the greatest calm, joy, peace, and lightness?
- What purpose will sound, harmonics and vibration create for me?

Take time to reflect before responding to these questions. There is no right or wrong response. At this point, do not judge your abilities but, instead, permit yourself to explore possibilities. You may have the answers, however, if you stay in the question and allow yourself the time and space to be open to more possibilities, you may find a deeper appreciation for why sound healing resonates with you. Your body and soul should be the guide to self-discovery and growth.

Exercises

Begin the journey to hear the silence of sound by performing this exercise at bedtime or upon awakening. At bedtime, be sure to turn off all electronic devices such as smartphones, televisions, and radios at least an hour prior. This will begin the process of training the mind not to be distracted. Lie down, close your eyes and listen to the sounds around you and inside of you. Hear your heartbeat, your breath, and the sounds of the room. Concentrate to hear the sounds and feel the vibration around you. For those with 'monkey mind, ' this exercise may be challenging. With practice, the ability to fully hear the sounds and feel the vibration will become easier. As it does, you can expand your awareness of sounds beyond the boundaries of the bedroom to space outside. As you expand beyond the physical boundaries of the room, you create greater awareness of the world. The more aware of the surrounding environment you become, the more conscious you become of what triggers thoughts and emotions. As you listen, what images and thoughts come to mind? Do those images and thoughts cause stress, anxiety or other emotions? Do you lose the ability to go beyond those thoughts and images? Journaling your experience is an important aspect of self-healing. The journal will assist you in facilitating the healing of others as it will serve as a point of reference to share with your clients.

The intent of the listening exercise was to begin pushing beyond your current capacity to hear and isolate sounds. What you may have experienced and may not have acknowledged is that you were also sensing the subtle vibrational energies. What did the body sense and what awareness may have been blocked by the mind? Take a moment to reflect on your experience. Read through your journal entries. Are there any hints of body awareness that have not been acknowledged? Were there sensations that you observed? Now, take the exercise to a different level. You have already learned how to become aware of your surroundings. Now it is time to determine if the thoughts, feelings, and emotions belong to you or somebody or something else. This is a great exercise to strengthen your ability to distinguish how your energy influences sound tools from the effects of someone else's energy. Be patient and refrain from second-guessing or doubting what you experience.

Are you ready to create a greater awareness of the power of sound and vibration? This exercise will require a space free of distractions. This exercise will use four senses: touch, sound, taste, and smell. If you own multiple sound tools, consider working with each one as each has its own vibrational energy. Start by sitting quietly and playing the instrument with your eyes closed or in low lighting. Feel the vibration of the instrument and allow the resonance of your body and the instrument to become one. Perform this exercise for at least 30 days. Doing this exercise over a long period will help you to learn how the resonance of the tool affects the dynamics of your mood and emotions. It will give you a sense of how that particular tool can change your energy. Knowing how your energy affects the sound, feeling, smell, and taste will help to distinguish if the change you sense during a healing session is yours, your client's or someone else's. As the symbiotic relationship with your sound tools grows, the need to play them to sense the shift in energy may diminish. Merely being in their presence can provide a sense about the world—the seen and unseen.

Going Beyond This Reality

What is meant by the unseen? In Hawaiian and Eastern cultures, reality has no boundary and is limited only by the rational mind. The rational mind creates a reality based on what can be perceived through the five senses: sight, sound, smell, touch, and taste. The brain is programmed to process and categorize information relative to our experiences. What if portals into a different awakened state—a state where time is no longer linear—can be opened by the resonance of a Himalayan singing bowl, a gong or a chant? What if the resonance of these sound tools challenged how our senses perceive our world? What if the edges between the dimensions could be bridged? What knowledge and gifts would become accessible? Only through direct experience with sound can you begin to gain an understanding of a multi-dimensional existence.

Becoming one with your sound tools and transcending the boundary of this earthly realm can be achieved as you journey down the path of healing. The more you play them, the more symbiotic the relationship becomes. Does this appear too far-fetched or unfathomable? A concept exists in some Eastern cultures that sound tools are sentient beings and have the capacity to communicate at multiple levels of consciousness. We are multi-dimensional beings yet, in many cases, have defined ourselves in a two or three-dimensional world which limits becoming aware of the invisible universe. How do you begin to develop the skill to receive more than the eyes perceive? The exercises in the previous section will begin to open the portals.

As the bridge between the seen and unseen manifests, you will begin to realize that the beauty and power of sound therapy do not lie in listening to the rhythmic beat or the sweetness of the instruments being played. The power of resonance exists within the silence that lies between the notes. In silence, you have the ability to transcend beyond the boundaries of the physical realm. What does that mean to be in the silence that lies between the sounds? Many people in Western culture are not introduced to silent meditation at an early age. They experience difficulty when attempting to sit quietly and allow the mind to dictate the body. Too often, we find our mind creating distractions such as making lists, planning what to do next, or reiterating an event of the day to avoid facing what is our greatest challenge. When you train your mind and body to release thoughts, emotions, feelings, and other distractions, you can begin to hear the silence. Sitting in silence, you begin to appreciate that "being still and doing nothing are two different things. "

Selecting Sound Tools

Any journey of self-discovery can become riddled with choices. You may begin to struggle with the question of how to afford the tools and training. By reflecting on what resonates with you and the responses to the questions posed earlier, you can develop a plan to guide the exploration of sound healing. The question that potentially has the greatest influence on your choice is: what sounds, tones and vibrations make your heart and body sing? Selection of sound tools is similar to a sacrosanct relationship. What techniques can be employed to select sound tools that will serve your highest level of consciousness? Having more does not equate to being more effective as a sound therapist or healer.

Here are some sound tools to consider:

- Gongs: Predominantly comprised of B20 alloy, this ancient sound tool penetrates every cell in the body. It may be used in a group or private setting.
- Himalayan Singing Bowls: Touted to be forged from seven sacred metals, they are believed to be bodhisattvas. Depending on the type and size, these can be used in a group or private setting.
- Crystal Singing Bowls: Made of 99.992% pure crushed quartz, they are tuned specifically to a single note, usually corresponding to one of the energy centers or chakras.

- Tuning Forks: An acoustic resonator in the form of a two-pronged fork with the prongs formed from a U-shaped bar, usually forged from metal. The length of the prongs determines the note.
- Drums: The world's oldest and most ubiquitous musical instruments. Eastern and Western culture use rhythmic beating to lull people into a trance-like state.

Here are some techniques that have been used to assist in the purchase of sound tools:

- Using a Pendulum: Hold a pendulum in your dominant hand. Allow its weight to hang and avoid swinging it in any direction. Hold or touch the sound tool. Ask, "Should I purchase this?" If the pendulum rotates in a clockwise direction, it is an indication the sound tool is right for you. If the pendulum rotates in a counter-clockwise direction, it indicates it is not right for you.
- Personal Budget: Setting a budget is highly advisable. The acquisition of any sound tool is based on the funds which are available. Perhaps sticking within your financial means will increase the likelihood you will refrain from making impulse purchases.
- Intuition: Gary Douglas and Dr. Dain Heer, founders of Access Consciousness, introduced the concept of 'heavy' or 'light.' Simply ask, "What will my life be like in five years if I buy you?" Is there a lightness when you ask the question? Then ask, "What will my life be like in five years if I don't buy you?" Is there

a greater sense of lightness or is it heavy? Remember, if it feels light, it is true for you. Try the same question but substitute five years with ten years.

There is no right or wrong way to select your sound tools. Simply do what is right for you. Trust in the knowledge that a single singing bowl can be as effective as a dozen singing bowls.

Working with Others

When you work with clients, allow the flow of energy to be unencumbered. Through the exploration of self, you learn to appreciate the commitment one requires to continue the journey of self-healing. You learn to have empathy for what others may experience as they work through the healing process. While it is key to listen to the vibrational energy of the sound tools to guide you during the session, do not discount the client's physical and emotional state. Establish where and what space your client is in and what is desired. The client's body and energetic response will serve as the primary guide during the session. Listening to how the body responds is essential in providing the client with what is necessary at that moment in time. I highly recommend you perform an intake before every session, even if you have seen the client in the past. The information you acquire during an intake period will help you understand what the client is capable of hearing and receiving. Beginning every session with a conversation builds the foundation and sets expectations. Ask open-ended questions.

- How are you feeling today?
- What is your expectation for today's session?

- Have there been any recent major events or changes in your life?
- What, if any, is the intention would you like me to hold during this session?

Meeting your client where they are, mentally and physically at the time of the session is essential to create the appropriate safe environment for them to relax and lower barriers to healing.

The world of sound, harmonics and vibrational healing is a magical one that can fill your life with joy and abundance. My wish for you is to have greater awareness and appreciation of our environment and the positive contribution we bring as healers.

CHAPTER

Seventeen

Your Healing Power
by Kira Murphy

KIRA MURPHY

Kira Murphy is a nationally and state board certified acupuncturist, with a Master of Science in Oriental medicine. The Master Graduate program lasted four and a half years with over 3,000 hours of training, 1,100 hours of which were hands-on clinical training. She owns Ki Healing Center in Denver, Colorado (Ki-Denver.com). Offering various types of healing treatments, both on-site and distant healing, Kira practices gentle acupuncture and esoteric healing. She incorporates various styles from which she has studied, such as Jin Shin Jyutsu, Reiki, Medical Qi Gong, Celtic Shamanism, 5 Element, and Quantum Energy medicine. One of her specialties, Kira can channel and draw a person's unique, one of a kind, sacred power symbol through meditation. Although Kira has been a healer since childhood, she has been formally practicing since about 2007. Kira has a daughter named Kiauna who is her inspiration. Kira has a heart full of gratitude for her parents for wholeheartedly supporting her.

Ki Healing Center
2238 S Broadway Denver CO 80210
303-709-4857
www.Ki-Denver.com

Your Healing Power
by Kira Murphy

What is your healing power? What can you offer to assist a person or heal within your life? How can you help others become happier and experience wholeness? Some people are born with a healing gift, and they use it from the day they are born. Some have dramatic events or awakenings and discover their gifts through events or even practice and study. While some people feel a connection to serve, lift up others and help people, they don't know what their gift is or how to find it! How do we know? How do we find it?

I want to switch gears and talk to you about pro-wrestling. Yes, the kind with eccentric, athletic, over-the-top characters such as Hulk Hogan, The Rock, and Andre the Giant! Why would I want to speak of this in a book about healing? Bear with me as I connect the dots and give you a new perspective on finding and utilizing your special healing gift. Gifts and healing powers come in many shapes and sizes and are often revealed in surprising ways. People who you may not label as healers can have just as much of a profound, positive and expanding reach as what we may stereotype as a typical healer. I want to inspire you to see the healer in all types of people, and expand your healing abilities to utilize skills you may not have categorized as healing tools. We all have many tools in our tool belt, and we may not even recognize them—yet.

I met and fell in love with a pro-wrestler named Mercury Matt Yaden. As an acupuncturist, energy healer, and person whose house is covered in crystals, tuning forks, and Chinese herbal remedies, one would imagine that we would be worlds apart! In my mind, I would have never thought it was possible for someone in that industry to be a healer or one of us lightworkers who help humanity shift into a higher frequency, lifting spirits, and causing momentum of positivity and inspiration. I love when I meet people who cause me to see things in a new light and shift and expand my paradigm. People like this man humble me and remind me of all the beautiful variety in this world and the multi-faceted way this universe operates. As I got to know him, I realized why our two completely different worlds were in complete harmony and why I consider him a healer just as much as I am.

Matt knows I am writing a chapter for a healing book, but I am certain he would never guess that he is mentioned in it. He wouldn't call himself a healer, just an everyday person. He'd probably say, "I do what I think is right, and try to be good to others." Nothing philosophical or metaphysical, just simple kindness, which is a purely loving way to live.

So many people touch others' lives and don't even realize it. It doesn't have to be labeled as "healer" or "healing" to impact people in an empowering and positively transformative way. On the outside, we might judge people or activities with a certain stereotype and imagine they must be on different pages, planes or planets than us. But, finding out the commonality in something or someone so different than you is truly at the root of all love, bonds, unity and human goodness—an important lesson that always makes us grow into wiser, deeper, people, not just the romantic love between two people. Love of life, love of a hobby, career, experience, or anything else where a person can fully express who they are without holding back.

What intrigued me so much about Matt was the amount of dedication and perseverance to being his authentic self. The way he committed to this and then attracted a group of people who had similar values and dreams is moving. The way he always includes all types of people and found creative ways to inspire and involve all levels of experience and ability inspires me.

The beauty of creating something out of nothing—out of a dream, out of thin air—is hard to put into words. This, to me, is what being alive is about. The result of pursuing a dream of living an authentic life and doing what you love has an effect on so many others' lives in positive ways—it is exponential. When I think of a healer, I think of these attributes. Not until I got to know Matt and his world did I understand the unlimited possibilities for a person to touch lives positively and how many ways a person can show up as a healer.

As a child, Matthew was bullied and tormented by other kids. They made his youth a living hell. While working at the mall, a couple of boys selling Beanie Babies at a kiosk nearby invited him to their house to do some pro-wrestling. That day, he found out he had a natural talent: he was good at wrestling. He experienced the amazing rush of doing something he loved with a group of supportive people. The spark was lit. He fell in love with pro-wrestling as a teen and never let that dream go. From a backyard ring, to owning a wrestling school and teaching others to wrestle, to hosting television shows and granting wishes for Make a Wish foundation kids, his heart, joy, belief and dedication manifested a dream that everyone told him was impossible.

When I asked Matt what his original dream was, he said, "To make it as a WWE superstar. I was given advice from Al Snow long ago to make a living in the business that I love, and the rest would take care of itself. So, my dream from that point on was to make a living doing what I love and help others achieve the same."

WWE seemed to always be out of reach. After many tryouts that were so close, Matt asked himself, "How can I continue to do what I love, work with people, and help others?" This was when he decided to do what everyone else told him was impossible and start a wrestling school.

When I first began dating Matt, his students were constantly telling me how wonderful of a person he is and how his school changed their lives. A student named Ted told me of when he was at his lowest point in life, depressed and out of shape. He said that after joining the school, he had something to look forward to and this motivated him to lose over 150 pounds.

I have never met a kinder group of people who care about and support each other. It is a gift to encourage those who have been bullied to be strong and confident, support those who are judged in daily life for being weird or different and create a community to offer what they love in their unity of teamwork. Providing an outlet and happiness to both students and a TV audience by being an authentic, genuine and caring teacher/leader with a full heart is one of the most inspiring things I can think of.

Why does this matter? When we think about healers, we might think about a shaman on top of a mountain, burning herbs and summoning spirit. This is one type of healer, but what is also needed right now in the world are individuals who focus on themselves being full in their hearts with authenticity, living their best life fully, with love and integrity. This type of existence translates to every person on their path and raises the vibration of the world. This elevates the collective consciousness and inspires a cascade of positive flow and healing. If we each did this, we could heal the planet.

In Matt's wrestling school, he enrolls students from ages six to sixty, female, male, transgender, straight, gay and anyone else in between. None of that matters. What does matter is the common goal of embracing one's character and becoming part of an entertainment team that brings people together to scream, cheer, get excited and escape the harsh realities of the day. No one is ever judged; a person's quirks and uniqueness are honored and celebrated! A willing mind and body are always welcomed, and creativity flourishes. When healers work with clients, we always accept everyone with no judgment, compassion, and view them through the eyes of God, seeing them perfect as they are and their wholeness and holiness as a huge gift of healing.

How amazing is it to openly invite all types of humans, honor each person's individuality and cherish the oddities that make us all different? When I am doing a healing session with a person, my goal is to honor and recognize all of these things!

By following your heart, passions, talents and gifts—even if they seem different from the "common" healing path—you are connecting to higher source and the vibration you tap into is unmatched. You have no idea the healing you create and the people's lives you will touch by following your heart and joy. It takes bravery to embody this in your life fully and go for it. The more people who do this, the more they will be inspired to live a full, happy life that is true to their core. Suffering, anxiety and physical pain occur because people are stifling their true joy, shunning their authentic illustration of self and keeping quiet when they have so much to share. Non-expression of who we truly are causes stagnation, and the body gives us painful or annoying symptoms to get our attention. Executing this free flow of life and embracing who we are is health and wellness.

Your healing modality does not have to be Acupuncture, Reiki, energy healing or a typical healing art to be considered a true healer. While I love these modalities so much so that I practice them myself, they are just a few to mention on an endless list of possibilities. The ability to join all types of people and help them bond over a common goal or interest is healing. Healing is helping a person to see their "weirdness" or what sets them apart as a beautiful gift and know that they are special. Connecting a person to their higher self, whether it is through energy medicine, inspiring confidence, releasing old thought patterns to grow or getting body-slammed in a wrestling ring and then popping up like a badass and embracing a crowd cheering with excitement—it is *all* healing.

The most important part of healing and helping others heal is connecting that person to who they truly are. It can happen with kindness, touch, action, ritual, certain protocols or your belief in someone or something. Your belief in a person can provide enough spark to reflect that belief back to them and start a cascade of positive beliefs and healing. Getting the system to shift back to its original state of Ohm, contentment and love physically changes the chemicals and cells in a human body, creating homeostasis and a healing response.

The point of explaining such spectrums is to show you that being a healer may not necessarily take eight years of traditional Chinese medical school, state board certifications or some lofty title or certificate. While all of these are absolutely fabulous, well-respected and deserved, you may have already honed your healing power and skill. You may have a way to give back and connect to others in such a positive and uplifting way that it is healing and beneficial to humanity.

Healing can come in many shapes and forms, in ways we haven't even fathomed. Following your heart, passion, love and not giving up on that part of your being will attract the right formula and people to create a positive response and healing for not only yourself, but all of those who cross your path. People will seek you out, and you will be able to provide them with authentic and true healing because you embody and you radiate healing. A shaman uses what they have around them in their environment and their relationship to higher self to create this connection. Anything can act as a healing modality which unites people or brings them into a positive state. There are so many ways to touch a person's life in a constructive or healing way through space, time, nature, and even technology that it shortens the distance to connect with a healer or someone in need.

What do you love and enjoy? What brings your happiness? What lights your fire? What moves you? What increases your energy? What speaks to you? If you'd like to be a healer and offer that to others, then you must find something that fills you up. Otherwise, you will constantly be drained and unhappy. Your cup needs to be refilled, and you should be vibrating high to have the ability to facilitate that lift to others. If you don't have it, how can you share or provoke it in others? Healing can occur in the most unexpected ways imaginable. If your passions are knitting and animals, maybe you can knit sweaters and blankets for a local animal shelter. Utilizing the craft you love, you can help animals and organizations which take care of animals in need. You will spread love, joy, peace, happiness and healing to all who receive your gifts. The possibilities and combinations are endless, and each person has a connection to something higher and a gift. You can figure that out by paying attention to your interests, skills, talents or even what boosts your energy and makes you feel lighter.

The world is ready and in need of new ways of healing. Maybe you connect the world and bring joy with pro-wrestling, or maybe you study the body and heal people by putting needles into acupuncture points on their bodies. As long as it is something you enjoy and feel passion towards, you will be a powerful influence and heal people who come into your field. So, let your freak flag fly and be your amazing self. That is your healing power!

CHAPTER

Eighteen

You First
by Linda Ingalls

LINDA INGALLS

Linda is a Certified Critical Care RN, Certified Emotion Code Practitioner, Berkeley Psychic Institute graduate, Healing Touch IV, Reiki Master, Intuitive Counselor / Coach, Energy Teacher and Author. She began speaking with her patients' spirits early in her ICU career. She will connect with your soul, subconscious and Source to guide your session, giving you what you want, what you need, and what Love knows is best for your highest good. Spirit will utilize her tools—create more if needed, to help you connect with the Love that you are so you can live a happier, more fulfilling life.

imlindai41@gmail.com, www.lindaingalls.com

Acknowledgments

First, I want to thank *Love* for everything. Second, I want to thank my sister, Sue Weiss and my friend, Leah Williams for their ongoing support, perceptions, and suggestions as my "beta-readers". Second, thanks to Carol Bundock, Christina A. Joy, Cindy Mizell, Diana Isabel Tibbs, Gail Jensen, Hannelore Jordt Evans, Lynn Frair, Lou Johnson

You First
by Linda Ingalls

Hi! Thank you for the work you do and for being you. I know you are kind-hearted and have a passionate desire to help people and the planet. Let's step this up by helping *you* first. Helping you first doesn't mean being selfish. Rather, it's an even higher service because you cannot give what you don't have. A well cannot provide water if it's empty or if its channel is narrowed. I am not talking about only clearing and raising your vibrations before a session; I am talking about clearing and *living* these life-flowing vibrations. Are you ready for this?

Let's start with some serious questions. Why are you a healer? What drives you? Do you receive healing when giving healing? Can you bring more to the table?

Many kind-hearted givers and healers *need* to fix, heal and give because underneath that kind-heartedness, they are too uncomfortable with someone else's discomfort. Is your empathy resonating so much that you can't feel okay until you fix whatever is going on? Do you tend to take on others' issues? Do you feel a need to protect yourself during a healing session or a need to cleanse afterward? I understand. Until you know a better way, keep doing that.

Good news! There is a better way, and when you know it, you will be an even better healer. One thing to do right now is to turn down your empathic dimmer switch to a level you can handle.

I don't practice or teach "protection." Instead, I want to empower you to understand your energy—how to manage it and your energetic communication—so you can know what is you, what is not you, and what to do about it. I want to empower you to choose the quality of energy you want to experience at any moment so that your world can open up and let life's playground expand. Instead of fear, I invite you to appreciate what I call divine darkness, sacred shadow, and luminous light, and learn how to proportion these so that you can create a life with a varied palette of colors and depth, a varied combination of notes and rhythms in your heart-song that will make your dance of life more fun and fulfilling. The more you can do this—be this—the more you will have to offer. I know you will receive healing while you are giving healing because you will be clearer to receive, have, and flow higher frequencies. Thus you will be refreshed.

I'm a retired registered nurse, six years in mental health, 32 in the Intensive Care Unit. Early in my ICU career, I began talking with my patients' spirits and became known for this. I helped my patients and they helped me to evolve; it was a bumpy path. Initially, I kept it a secret until one day, I threatened to quit if I wasn't allowed to take care of my patient, Abigail, because her spirit told me she was going into a life or death crisis and I needed to help her through it. That didn't go over well. After much deliberation, they let me stay. She went into crisis and I helped her spirit choose, in each moment, whether to live or pass on. She lived, eventually left the ICU; and I was out of the spiritual closet.

Another turning point was with Mamie. I cared for her, spoke with her spirit and shared it with her family. She got better and left the ICU. A year later, she was back and in worse condition. The family remembered me. I decided to say hello to Mamie's spirit again. In my mind, I saw her standing about eight feet from me.

She said, "Don't talk to me, Linda. I don't want to hear anything you have to say."

I knew she was afraid of dying. I replied, "No worries. I'm just going to stand here and love you." When I said that, my whole spiritual body lit up and I felt immense love for her. I saw a spot of *love and light* in her body, so I put my attention there. The spot amplified! Soon, she was leaning toward me, reaching toward me, stepping toward me, and then hugging my waist. She was irresistibly drawn to the vibrations of *love and light* which I was holding for her. At that moment, a light appeared, and a large group of spirits were giggling and calling for her. She knew them and wanted to be with them. (See these stories in my book, *I May Be Crazy, But It's All Good*.)

I saw that the foundation for healing is to hold the vibrations of *love and light* so that those same vibrations in the "healee" (person receiving the healing) would automatically tune in, like tuning one guitar string to another. And by putting my attention on those life-flowing vibrations, they amplified. Then, I saw an image of a bonfire and people bringing their torches to be lit. Many torches burned out when they left so they came back to relight them. Some of the torches stayed lit for a while then dwindled out. Some stayed lit and not only continued to burn brightly, but they were also able to light other torches. In this same way, our healees will resonate with these wellness-causing, higher vibrations to the degree that they can. It may be a temporary tune-up that alleviates symptoms for a bit. It may be a tune-up that removes the current "dis-ease" and gives them a taste of possibility. But life happens, they forget, and another dis-ease manifests later. Or, it could be this tune-up was all they needed to cause a transformational step-up. It's part of their path to make these choices. That can be hard for healers to watch. We feel what others feel. This may trigger our empathy into judging that something needs to be fixed. We may lose our higher vibrational consciousness and start spinning out in uncontrolled empathy, taking on others' issues, losing ourselves, and eventually, burning out.

I learned I could hold these vibrations of *love and light* while meeting a person at their level. I could get on my knees with them, hold them and cry with them. They would eventually tune in to the higher vibrations I was holding for them. Instead of using my empathy, I used compassion. I did this by understanding energy, which taught me how to set my "bio-vibe," how to know when I was out of it, what took me out of it, what to do about it, and how to get it back. I have the consciousness and freedom to shift, knowing that sometimes healing will be a *do it for* them healing, and sometimes a *do it with* them healing. Sometimes it's teaching them a *do it yourself* healing, and sometimes it's everything. Sometimes it's only coaching. Whatever modality of healing work you do, you will lift it and yourself higher if you understand and manage your energy.

The following is a truncated excerpt and exercise of one of the first things I teach to all my students:

"Everything is energy, and you are in constant comm-unication with it. You all have experienced feeling the 'vibe' of a person, place or situation and instinctively know whether you feel comfortable with it or not. Are you triggered? Is a part of you resonating with a vibe you don't want? You can surround yourself in white light, sage, religious symbols, and 'talk to the hand,' but you cannot avoid interfacing with the energy around you. Also, there is no vault to hide the energy of your emotions and thoughts. There is no separation between your energy and others. So, what do you do? It's quite easy. The first step is in knowing your energy and how to set the vibe you want to live. I call it creating your bio-vibe. Let's break it down into its parts so you know how to get back when you are not there."

Creating Your Bio-Vibe:

A. **Grounding**: Grounding gives you choice. It's the first tool to know and use in energy awareness and management. Elements to know:

1. Response vs. Reaction: Our brain is our Central Nervous System, from which two nerve pathways connect with all parts of our body: the Parasympathetic, our "calm" pathway, and the Sympathetic, our "fight or flight" pathway. If you stepped off a curb and a cyclist whizzed past, you would experience an instant surge of energy. The healthy response is for your body to jump back onto the curb. The unhealthy reaction is to chase the cyclist and scream obscenities at him. A reaction is like playing pinball; once that ball is launched, it's out of control.

2. Surging is a spike in energy. The third prong on a 3-prong plug is the ground. It keeps your

appliances from blowing out by giving electricity a safe path to the Earth in case of a problem or surge in the system.

3. "Earthing" is a technique where you put your bare feet on the ground for two hours a day. The National Institute of Health has studies which prove connecting to the Earth is beneficial for the body.

4. Grounding Cord: You learned the fact that everything is energy, and there is no barrier to its flow; that form follows thought; and that your intention gives direction and purpose to the flow of your energy. So, you can create your energetic connection to the Earth, your grounding cord, simply by imagining and intending it to be so.

Exercise:

Close your eyes and, using your imagination, create a connection that goes from your tailbone down into the Earth. It could be an anchor, a waterfall, a tree root or whatever you want. It only takes a moment to imagine it. Then breathe into it, feel it, allow your energy to connect and flow into the Earth.

Stay grounded and open your eyes. How did that feel? Some folks say they feel more present and connected, not "floaty." You may not have noticed any changes, and that's okay.

Exercise:

Close your eyes and say hello to your grounding cord. Saying "hello" means you put your attention there and acknowledge it. Now, disconnect your grounding cord from your tailbone and—poof! It's gone. Experience how it feels to be ungrounded and disconnected from the Earth.

Now, create a new grounding cord. It can be exactly like the last one, or it can be a new image. Then breathe into it and feel it.

Stay grounded and open your eyes. Did you feel a difference between being grounded and not grounded? Being grounded brings in the vibrations of stability and security. Please stay grounded as we move forward.

Grounding can also be your emergency response. When you have pain (physical, emotional, mental or spiritual), there is always secondary energy added to it. First, there's the pain. Then you react. "Oh my God! What is this? What should I do? See a doctor? Call 911? Call in sick?" This is a surge of secondary energy added to the pain stimuli. Imagine an extension of your grounding cord connecting to wherever the pain is and let all the energy go down your grounding cord. This switches you from reaction to response mode and allows you to *choose* your response.

B. **Centering**: Centering is putting your attention within your core, into your place of peace.

Exercise:

Close your eyes and say hello to your grounding cord. Now, use your imagination and create a peaceful place within your core. (Form follows thought.) Think of it as the eye of a hurricane; the hurricane is your life, thoughts, body, and emotions. Enjoy being in peace.

Now stay grounded, centered and open your eyes.

I once worked with a nurse who did not know any of these things, but she was a naturally grounded, centered and experienced nurse. She'd been taking care of a woman for a while in the ICU. One morning, her patient's heart stopped. The nurse jumped onto the bed, began CPR, and called a Code Blue. This was a teaching hospital so people came to learn from this experience. The nurse elected to continue doing CPR while assigning people various jobs and supervising the doctor, too. I saw a tear traveling down her cheek. This nurse was aware of what was happening within herself while she was taking care of business.

Exercise:

Close your eyes. Say hello to your grounding cord and be in your center. See if you can be aware of what you are experiencing within yourself while, at the same time, being aware of what is happening around you—the temperature in the room, your butt in the seat, any noises.

Stay grounded, centered, and open your eyes. Was your attention drifting in and out? If so, this is normal. With practice, it happens so fast it's as if you are aware of everything at once. With grounding and centering, we have the vibrations of stability, security, and peace. Please stay grounded and centered as we continue.

C. **Happy Place**: The happy place is the "smile within." It's anything that automatically makes you smile when you think of it. It can be the thought of a place, person, thing, or even a joke that always cracks you up.

Exercise:

Say hello to your grounding cord and be in your center. Create a space within your center for your happy place and put a happy thought into it. You can have as many happy thoughts as you want; you can change them as often as you wish. Enjoy playing in your happy place.

Stay grounded, centered, in your happy place, and open your eyes. How are you feeling? Are you smiling? You have just added the vibration of happiness to your vibrations of stability, security and peace.

D. **Alignment**: Do you believe in a higher power? You don't need to for this. Whether you believe in a higher power or not, whether you're currently getting along with your higher power or not, you can tune in to the high-frequency vibrations of *love, joy, and connection to all.*

Exercise:

Say hello to your grounding cord, be in your center and happy place. Now, invite those high frequencies of love, joy, and connection to all into your happy place to be with you. Allow them to lift your happy place even higher.

How are you feeling? Does it feel good? You now have the vibrations of *stability, security, peace, happiness, joy, love, and connection to all.* Now stay grounded, centered, in your happy place, aligned and connected with your higher power or higher vibrations and open your eyes.

You have just set your bio-vibe! When you know your vibe, you will know when you are not there and the first things to do: ground, center, happy place, and align.

Understanding what takes you out of your bio-vibe and ways to deal with that is another topic in class.

One way I utilize my bio-vibe is when choosing which direction to take. I will act like a human compass. I stand up, feel my awesome bio-vibe, and say, "If I choose this direction, how does that feel?" Then I turn a little to the right. "Oh no! That took me right out of my vibe!" I *turn back* into my good feeling bio-vibe. Then I say, "How about choosing this direction? How does it feel?" Then, I turn a little to the left. "Well, it isn't bad, but it doesn't feel as good as my bio-vibe." So, I turn back into my bio-vibe. Then I will keep turning into and out of different directional choices until I find the one that feels exactly like my bio-vibe and *that* will be the direction I choose to go into because I always want to feel these vibrations. You can use this vibe to meditate or when trying to sleep. I am inviting you to *live* this vibe.

CHAPTER

Nineteen

Tips And Thoughts About Having A Healing Practice
by Marion Andrews

MARION ANDREWS

Bestselling author, Marion Andrews, strives to impart the knowledge and wisdom she has gained through classes, certifications and volunteer leadership positions. Teaching comes naturally to her. Marion has chosen to use Reiki as the way to heal your inner self as well as help with your physical health. Marion can offer you relaxing, restorative Reiki in person or via distant energy work and online meditation classes, from beginner to deep practice. If you are ready to take a clear look at your life, book some life coaching sessions.

marion@marionandrews.com

www.chrysaliswellnesscenter.com

www.facebook.com/ChrysalisWellnessCenter

Acknowledgments

Michelle Forsyth, my daughter who is my heart, best critic and timekeeper. Cyndy Paxton RMT, my master teacher and helper in all that is Reiki. Sharon Quill, my sweet, southern friend who motivates me and laughs with me. Vicki Snyder Young, a talented reader, healer and friend who encourages me every time we are together. Dave Andrews, my husband who has grown so much in this journey with me.

Tips and Thoughts on Having a Healing Practice
By Marion Andrews

In the beginning: Reluctant? Skeptical? Those were the words that certainly applied to me. I discovered Reiki on a journey, searching for deeper spiritual roots. I was looking for ways to enhance my spirituality and my connection to the universe. I was guided to a Reiki master through a Google search. She invited me to try my first session of Reiki. I didn't know anything about Reiki and was hesitant about this "woo-woo" stuff. After one treatment, I knew I wanted to be a part of the beautiful energy that I experienced at the center. I am also a lover of learning and immediately wanted to learn more! I registered for the Reiki 1 and 2 classes in the next few months.

At that time, I was having some health issues that had not been identified. Within a month of this first treatment, I was given the diagnosis of stage four colon cancer, had major surgery and was scheduled to begin chemotherapy. As I look back, I can see that I was divinely guided through all of this. I was on a path to fulfill my purpose in a new and exciting way. My Reiki master attuned me to Reiki 1 so that I could give myself treatments over the next months of chemo. I also began journaling and meditating at this same time. At first, I did the Reiki only occasionally, and all these things were done with a doubting attitude and not much credence. But I was desperate to be healthy again.

You or your clients may have felt the same way in the beginning. Guess what? It doesn't matter. The energy is there, working to heal you. The intention is to move out negative energy and bring in some positive healing vibes. That is exactly what happens.

This is important! You and I are not healers. The energy from spirit/God/universe is the healer. You and I are the conduits for that healing energy. I was so relieved when I realized this. When I was healthier, I completed the Reiki classes. Over the next three years, cancer returned again and again, and my belief and trust in the healing energy grew each time I defeated that nasty disease. I am now happy to say that I have completed one year of being cancer-free. Our training and knowledge certainly allow us to help in many ways. You will find that as you experience opportunities to work with different clients and learn other modalities, your confidence will grow. You will have tools in your toolbox and spirit has ways to affect healing in others.

Becoming Serious About This

I had been looking for my life purpose for as long as I can remember. What am I supposed to be doing here on earth? Am I walking on my path? Am I fulfilling the contract I made with the universe? I have asked all sorts of people over my lifetime. When I faced what could be a life-threatening disease, I thought, "Okay, it's time to get serious. What am I supposed to be learning here?" The answer came to me loud and clear while I was meditating one day. My purpose was to teach and to heal. Since I had benefitted so much from the healing energy of Reiki, I decided it would be my main way of helping others to heal. I was attuned as a Reiki master and opened a wellness center.

Here I am! I have finished my master training. All that hard work is done. We have a beautiful, welcoming place. The colors are soothing, yet alive with energy. The healing/treatment room is ready with fresh, clean sheets. The music is softly playing. Angels are lined up, ready to assist as they are asked. Open the doors! Let the people in!

Wait a minute! Where are the people? Does this sound familiar? Yes, we need to do some preparatory work to bring in clients. The most important things here are intention and attitude. You need a sincere desire to help others as your primary goal. In the planning and operating of your business, use the energy modality that you are trained in. Positive things happen when you are in this high vibrational flow.

Some of the things that I did:

- Offer free 15-minute sessions at company employee health days.
- These are like a fair with various vendors providing services for the employees. It is usually held right in the company's facility. All employees are encouraged to take an hour or two to visit the area. Services like Reiki, massages, fitness and healthy foods are featured. I offer a discount on a full service if booked and paid for at the event.
- Classes at the YMCA or similar organizations
- Senior workshops
- Trade shows, especially those geared to women's health and spirituality

- Speaking at club meetings
- Flyers and notices in the immediate business area
- A website to explain what I do and to book clients

How to Retain Clients

The most effective way to retain a good client base is simple: *treat them exactly like you want to be treated.* I know, it's the old golden rule again. Do unto others as you want others to do unto you. In this case, it is the best formula.

Things that work:

- Confirming the appointment. Today there are programs that you can use to do this automatically. I use email and text. I send an email right after the appointment is booked with the details. Then 24 hours before, I follow that with a text message.
- Be ready for them when they arrive. I generally plan to be completely ready 10-15 minutes before the appointment time. Usually, I prepare the room with energy and then do a 5-minute meditation to prepare myself. I ask all my spirit helpers to be there to boost the energy and make sure that the client is getting what they need from me. Again, it is such a wonderful feeling to know that I am not alone in this healing work. I am a willing channel for this energy flow.
- In the opening minutes of the appointment, gather the important information that you will need. Listen to your client. I keep a file for each person with the initial release forms and other paperwork. I note any personal details that are shared. I also note their preferences for the way they like the table or chair

that I am using. The next time they come in, I have those little things ready. The clients are opening their personal and vulnerable side to you. Treat them gently and with respect.

- Make sure that the client is comfortable. Some people prefer a pillow on the treatment table, others do not. I have extra sheets and blankets handy to accommodate their needs.

- Make sure that they know where the restrooms are and anything else that they might need. Offer something to drink. I always offer water as it is important to flush out the system after an energy treatment.

- Suggest booking their next treatment at the end of the appointment. I also offer a discount if they buy three sessions at once. For instance, each Reiki session is $70 for one hour. I offer three prepaid sessions for a discounted price of $180.

- Sending a thank you note or a small card is a great way to show the client that you do appreciate the opportunity to help them heal. Studies show that people respond to a hand-written note/card more than an electronic one. Do something special for them.

- In that same vein, sending a birthday card by snail mail is a sweet thing to do and appreciated by the client. People do not get physical cards in the world of texts, emails and tweets. Be different. Be remembered. I like to pick a theme and stay with that. For instance, if they are a cat lover, I will send something with a kitty on it. Of course, I include all my business information and two business cards as well.

- Ask for referrals. I do not do this until after the second or third appointment. I want them to feel positive results, then they will want to share the experience with their friends and family.

Distant Reiki or Any Energy Healing

This is an effective way to help. It takes discipline to accomplish this. It is worth it to your client. I belong to a group of healers that do distant energy healing every Monday night. Anyone can put their name on a list asking for healing energy. There are various modalities represented. The power of the combined energy is amazing.

Personal Development

Immerse yourself in your modality. Live with it every day. It feels so good to enjoy a session of healing. Learn as much as you can about it. Become a student of history and read stories about how others were helped. Attend as many functions as you can.

I participate in an event called a Reiki share. Several Reiki practitioners meet monthly for 2-3 hours. We catch up and share what has been happening in our lives. Then we each have 20 minutes of healing at the hands of two or more. We each have a turn on the table, and all participate in the giving of healing energy. It was through the feedback at these events that my confidence and ability grew. Others told me how vibrant they felt after my giving them a treatment, I then felt assured when out talking to prospective clients.

Never stop learning and growing. The universe will open all sorts of doors for you. Be trusting and brave! Walk through. I have contributed to four books on a variety of topics in the past year. I have also authored a guided journal with my daughter. None of these things **would** have been possible if I had ignored the invitation to try energy healing.

Ways to Keep your Mojo

Teach. Practice. Share. Meditate. Journal.

If you are qualified as a teacher with energy work, then teach! Even when you don't have students, practice teaching. Write the plan for a training day. Then fill in the script. Then practice. When you were young, did you ever play "school?" I was several years younger than my siblings, and we lived on a farm away from any neighbors, so I played alone a lot of the time. I would set up make-believe desks with cardboard boxes, set dolls or stuffed animals as students in them and I would teach! Whenever my cousins came to visit, we played school! Do this same rehearsing now. Before you can attune someone in Reiki, you must have practiced so you can carry out the ritual with great intention and peace. The energy again does the real work, but we need to do our part of preparation. This has the two-fold advantage of making the universe/spirit/angels aware of your desire and intention. Then the students will come. Do the same for any of the treatments or workshops you offer.

Meditate

One of the most valuable tools in your healing business is meditation. The time spent in the quiet environs of your mind is an amazing adventure. In this quiet, I hear the answers or prods from the universe, archangels and my spirit guides. Sometimes they are the softest whispers, and I need to be tuned in. Sometimes they are loud and clear, and I am beyond grateful that I have this guidance. Sometimes I am surprised with their presence. Sometimes they whisper encouragement or pour out love. Is it hard to believe? Yes, sometimes it is! Our job is not to figure out the details, but to be open to what is happening around us. Do you ever get an urge to go to a certain store or place? Follow that lead. See what happens. Your intention as a healer is to sincerely help others. This intention and desire will attract those who need our help. I firmly believe that there is no competition in this world of healing. I trust that those whom I am here to help will find me. I need to be out and about. I need to be living with the expectation of the divine plan unfolding. Meditation helps me with all these attitudes.

Gratitude

An attitude of gratitude *must* be cultivated to reap the benefits of an energy healing practice.

I say "must" here because it is crucial to your success in this field. It is crucial to success in any field but especially one that aligns so closely with the universe. We attract ideas and people who are on the same vibration. Oprah Winfrey says, "Gratitude elevates your life to a higher frequency."

A practice I highly recommend is keeping a gratitude journal. Create an attractive header for the page in your journal. Add to it every morning, and then again, each evening. Begin your day by saying something like, "I am so happy and grateful now that I am.... Thank you, angels/God/spirit for bringing this into my life."

The best advice I can give is to be present and be open. See everything with wonder and mystery.

An Exercise with a Different Type of Meditation

Five-Minute Moving Meditation

This is my "go-to" meditation before every treatment, every talk, and I use this almost every day. You can use this to gather some quick energy, to settle and ground yourself, or to feel invigorated.

Standing with your hands in gassho position *(hands in prayer position, hands together, thumbs over heart chakra)*, regulate your breath with a few deep breaths, allowing your natural breathing rhythm to take over.

Now, standing comfortably, with your feet a bit apart, hold your hands about 8-10 inches apart at the height of your heart chakra.

Imagine a bright, white light of energy going between your palms.

1st affirmation

Breathe in while saying, "I am open and receptive to all that is for my highest good," while raising arms up.

Now, turning your palms out, breathe out.

Bring your arms to your sides.

Breathing in, raise the hands, palms down, to the heart chakra.

Now exhale while saying, "And I trust the process of the universe" while pushing the hands down and the energy down to connect with the earth.

Repeat two more times.

2nd affirmation

Same posture as above.

Breathe in and say, "I establish my divine purpose here on earth," while raising the arms up.

Now, turning your palms out, breathe out.

Bring your arms to your sides.

Breathing in, raise the hands, palms down, to the heart chakra.

Now push the air out, pushing the hands down and the energy down to connect with the earth.

Repeat two more times.

3rd affirmation

Same posture as above.

Breathe in and say, "I accomplish my divine purpose here on earth" while raising the arms up.

Now, turning your palms out, breathe out.

Bring your arms to your sides.

Breathing in, raise the hands, palms down, to the heart chakra.

Now push the air out, pushing the hands down and the energy down to connect with the earth.

Repeat two more times.

CHAPTER

Twenty

Divine Love Is The Ultimate Super Power
by Monica Brown

MONICA BROWN

Monica is a speaker, coach and author. She helps moms figure out what makes them happy so that they can be balanced, joyful moms and women. She offers workshops, retreats and private mentoring. Monica's passions are being a holistic, happy mama to her children, loving everyone in her path, traveling the world and spending time exploring and playing in nature.

How to contact Monica:

www.bliss-soul.com

www.Facebook/MonicaBrownBliss

www.LinkedIn.com/in/Monica-brown-3703022

Acknowledgments

My deepest appreciation to Kyra Schaefer for her grace, wisdom, support, inspiration and invitation into the world of authorship.

Divine Love is the Ultimate Super Power
by Monica Brown

Have you felt ill or emotionally upset and actively tried to make yourself feel better only to realize later that it was someone else's illness or disturbance? Have you experienced surreal things that made you think that you are crazy? Have you had a sense of light coming out of your hands or out of your heart? Have you noticed plants, animals or people become healthier when you touch them or think loving thoughts about them? Do these things scare you or thrill you?

I am here to tell you that you are not alone. When I first discovered that I was open to these experiences, I felt wonder, fear, confusion, curiosity, excitement, disbelief, mystified, energized, full of life, unworthy and a recognition of truth. I am going to share with you a few things that I experienced as I was coming into this awareness of my healing gifts.

I am in class and can't wait to leave. My stomach is cramping. I become aware that this pain may not be mine. The instructor looks uncomfortable, and I sense that this discomfort is *his* pain. When class is finally over and I drive away, my stomach relaxes. By the time I arrive home, I feel like me again—healthy.

I watch with curiosity as a four inch tall, human-shaped, violet-winged light flutters around the head of my sleeping infant a foot and a half away. What the what? That can't be real! I close my eyes. I open my eyes. Still there. Wonder takes over. What are you? It moves from my infant to my toddler, and lastly, to my preschooler. It seems to be checking on them. I am astonished. What is it doing? It sees me in the dark, too. I feel like it is irritated that I can see it, but it continues. In the quiet darkness, I ask, "What are you?"

At my first appointment with my naturopathic physician, I am surprised to learn that she is also a Shaman. I feel terrified, confused and curious as she demonstrates she can hear my thoughts. She tells me that I have the ability to clear my house. She instructs me how. A few nights later when the paranormal intensifies, I try to take my house back by clearing it. I am intimidated and afraid. I end up running from the "ghosts" in my home and, weeks later, the Shaman clears my house.

I'm meditating in my garden. I am barely aware that I have a body. My guidance system alerts. Across the street, my neighbor is at his mailbox. Before I know what has happened, a part of me flashes out of my body and is located behind him. Violet-lighted hands whoosh onto his mid and lower back and I hear, "His kidney stones are gone."

When a person becomes acutely aware of their psychic senses or healing abilities, it can be overwhelming, exciting, confusing, wondrous or scary.

When this happened for me, I sought guidance from spiritual teachers and books. One of the instructions that I heard repeatedly was "protect your field." I followed their instructions. Although it worked, it was not foolproof. I believe protection is defensive and based in fear.

I want you to know that you have unlimited skills and ways to manage your field, only limited by your imagination. I believe that as you develop deep trust in your inner guidance system that you will find the best way for yourself, a way that allows you to be keenly aware of energy and know its origination, intent and purpose. You will know what belongs to you, what belongs to others and if it is your place or not to heal it. It is a journey.

I wish to share with you tools to build your field and be your field. I invite you to let go of protection as your primary way to insulate yourself from the energy outside of you. I wish to remind you that *you originate in love and oneness.* You are and have always been one with the Divine, Source, God, Spirit, (whatever you believe to be your greater power). Your field and your connection to the *divine* is the most powerful "protection" that you have available.

Love is the ultimate superpower; it heals all wounds and shifts the world around you. The greater your connection to the *divine* and the more that you allow the loving energy of the *divine* to flow into you and emanate from you, the more powerful your energy field will be from the inside out. You can let the *divine* fill you up and flood into your field and out into the world around you. When you are connected to your higher power, you will live with more grace, ease, happiness and good health, and you will be less affected by the energy pool and waves of consciousness that you swim in. Your psychic abilities will be clearer and your healing capacity will be greater.

Source flowing through you continuously is powerful. As you expand your connection, you may find yourself living in sustainable comfort, peace, knowing, joy, safety and love; aware of the energy and thought forms of others, yet unaffected by them.

Opening a flow to your *divine* guidance system and being aware of it is an art and a science. You can open and expand your channels and capacity to be one with the *divine*. If you keep moving towards that goal, your awareness will expand. The greater your connection to your internal source and the more that you are willing to allow the *divine* to fill you up continuously, the easier life becomes.

Being centered and grounded is a vital component of perceiving your connection to *your divine source*. It allows you to be an open channel for the *divine* to fill you up and allows you to be more aware of your energy and *divine* guidance than the energy of people and situations outside of you.

Being centered and grounded is your energy being in your body. It enables you to discern what belongs to you and what doesn't. It enhances your ability to be a powerful transmitter of loving energy. A strong, consistent electrical current needs a steady, consistent ground to produce a powerful and consistent electrical volt.

When you are centered inside of your energy, you are aware of your thoughts, feelings and energy, separately from that of other people. This is a powerful place to be. You know what originates in you, what belongs to someone else and how to make choices that honor you.

What does it feel like to be grounded and centered?

You are aware of your body. You feel your feet on the ground. You feel stable like there is a column from above your head that comes down through your body and out from your feet. Your breath is full, deep, slow and regulated. Your mind is quiet and alert. You feel focused and relaxed, simultaneously.

What does it look like when you are grounded and centered?

Others will perceive you as being patient, present, powerful, calm, gracious, decisive, clear, compassionate, kind, creative and taking appropriate action when necessary. You see solutions that others don't see.

How grounded are you?

Are you a busy bee? If you can't or don't want to be still and need to have a million things to do, or move about at a quick pace, ask yourself, "Why?"

What are you avoiding? A situation? Are you afraid to feel? Have you been this way most of your life because you don't trust life or don't want to be in your body due to emotional pain or discomfort?

If you said yes to any of the above questions, do your inner work. Grow your ability to feel safe and supported by the *divine* in your life.

How centered are you?

Can you easily decide yes or no when someone asks you to do something without regretting the answer or the commitment, then or later?

If not, your energy may be scattered or your energy may be enmeshing with the person who is making the request. If you enmesh, you are more likely to either respond with what they want (people-pleasing) or how they expect you to respond instead of honoring yourself.

Simple ways to ground and center.

Nature. Spend time outdoors being inactive. Run, hike, walk or bike, but then, busy bee, let yourself sit for a few minutes also or lay out on that flat rock.

Water. Get into the ocean, the river, the lake and even a warm bath. If you opt for the warm bath, throw in at least one cup of Epsom salt. The body likes magnesium. It supports physiological relaxation, purification and assists with energetic clearing. Being immersed in warm water has been shown to increase oxytocin levels—now that is *divine*! Drink filtered water, lots of it.

Eye Contact. When you are engaged in listening or speaking, make eye contact with the other person. Listen fully. This keeps you in your body and present in the moment.

Pleasure. Purposely allow yourself physical pleasures. Some ways to do this are movement (dancing, biking, running, stretching, massage), enjoying scents (flowers, food, essential oils), taste by enjoying great meals, sensual and sexual pleasure. All these things tune you and your body together in positive and pleasant ways. If you like to escape your body, I recommend making your body an enjoyable place to experience and build safety and self-trust.

Your Feet. Walk barefoot and feel the carpet, the dirt, the grass or whatever surface is under you. Notice the temperature, the texture and the feel. Now relax your feet. Drop your shoulders down, let your feet feel steady and connect to the surface under you. Gently and lovingly massage your feet or get a foot massage. Send yourself the message that it is safe to bring all of yourself into your body by creating a sensation at the bottom of the feet and the tips of the toes. When you are grounded and centered, you are aware of your body, you feel your feet on the ground and you feel stable, as if you are a column from top to bottom. Your breath is full, deep, slow and regulated. Your mind is quiet and alert. You feel focused and relaxed, simultaneously.

Being One with the Divine

You can train your physical, mental, emotional and energetic systems to stay present with the *divine* throughout your day regardless of what you are doing, where you are going or who you are with.

What does it feel like to be fully connected to source?

This is personal and dependent upon your physical makeup and how you integrate your nonphysical *divine* being with your physical being. The following is an example of what you may experience physically. Your body will feel relaxed. You may feel a connection as fullness in your heart; light pressure, as if someone is gently touching your forehead and tingling; light pressure on the scalp of your head, allowing a deep, relaxed expansion.

Emotionally, you may feel (maybe even deeply), but you will not be afraid. You will feel safe even when circumstances around you aren't what your mind thinks are safe. You may feel love, compassion, acceptance, peace, joy, bliss and gratitude.

How do you act when you are connected?

While being connected, it is easier to think, speak and act with clarity, grace, love, kindness, compassion, appreciation, firmness and invincibility. Your ability to be peacefully steadfast in the face of chaos becomes unwavering. Your field, emanating the higher energies of the *divine,* will affect the people, places and situations around you in ways that allow for better outcomes for yourself and others. The *divine* is absolute love. When love is present in every nook and cranny of your mind, your body, your emotions and your field—you don't need protection. You are allowing the *divine* to choose through you the highest path, possibility and outcome for the highest good of all.

A meditation practice to ground, center and expand your connection to the *divine*:

Sit in an upright position and close your eyes. Feel your feet firmly on the ground and your bottom on the chair. Become aware of your breath. Have the intention to relax your body. Relax every muscle in your body. Allow your mind to relax and become quiet by having it observe your breath. Let go of all physical tension, layer by layer.

Bring your awareness to your fourth chakra. Your fourth chakra resides in and around your physical heart and body. Your fourth chakra is called "Anahata" in Sanskrit, which means "unhurt, unstruck, unbeaten." *This is your center of purity and love.*

With your attention on your heart chakra, allow your body to be relaxed. Allow your breath to flow naturally. Your breath may become deeper, fuller and more rhythmic as you continue to relax.

With your awareness at your heart chakra and your body relaxed, be loosely aware of the form of your body. Allow your mind to continue to quiet. Feel your heart and the appreciation and love that resides there.

With each breath, continue to relax. Keep your awareness on your fourth chakra and allow yourself to feel the wholeness, love, kindness, patience, joy, bliss and peace that reside within your heart and within the *divine*.

Now let go of awareness of your physical form. It is possible that in this deep, relaxed state that your breath may quiet and stop for periods of time. You are completely safe if this naturally occurs. In deep union with the *divine*, less breath is needed.

Allow yourself to be present in this experience and let the *divine* know that you intend to be aware of your connection in quiet times and in daily life. *Invite the divine to be continually present in your life and your awareness*: filling you, nurturing you, loving you, guiding you, keeping you safe and working through you.

Trust your process and be clear in your intention to be "bio-available" for the *divine*.

Sit until you feel full and complete.

Before opening your eyes, become aware of the room. Acknowledge your connection to the *divine*. Feel what your connection feels like.

Now, feel your feet firmly and ground by imagining that you have roots of light growing from your feet or your earth energy field down into the ground. Feel the roots providing you stability while still allowing you the freedom to move.

Slowly begin to wiggle your fingers and toes. Gently stretch and move your body, allowing all of your being to come back into your physical form. When you are ready, open your eyes.

CHAPTER

Twenty-One

Getting Your Answer
In Ten Minutes
by Sherry Anshara

SHERRY ANSHARA

Sherry Anshara is an international bestselling author, professional speaker, former radio host of "Conscious Healing", and contributing writer to national and international publications on the subject of the Anshara Method of Accelerated Healing & Abundance and overall wellness. Sherry Anshara utilizes her experience and expertise as a Medical Intuitive and Intuitive Business Coach as the foundation of her groundbreaking work with Cellular Memory, which she calls the Anshara Method.

Through the Anshara Method, you access your Cellular Memories which hold the root causes of your symptoms— whether mental, physical, emotional, spiritual, or financial. Sherry Anshara created these systematic processes so you can rid yourself of unwanted limitations, restrictions, negative thought patterns, and toxic behaviors. Sherry Anshara guides you to heal at the cellular level so you enjoy health, wellness, and abundance in every area of your life.

Acknowledgments

Mariah Thompson, Wind Ohmoto, Myrna Solano, Jana Fiero, Elonna Tinkle

Getting Your Answer
in 10 Minutes
by Sherry Anshara

W hat? In ten minutes? Is this possible? Can I truly get the answer I've been seeking for who knows how long to heal this deep-seated physical or emotional issue? Yes!

It will take longer to read this chapter than to use my method to get your answer! I will share with you the basics of the method I created through my five near-death experiences to heal my broken back, neck and smashed head which I continued to develop as a Medical Intuitive for 28 years, assisting thousands of people worldwide in healing their bodies and their lives of ailments and traumas.

Why does healing seem to take a long time? Is this the truth? Or is it a limited belief system which has been perpetuated for far too many years? Could the idea of taking a long time to heal your core issues have begun with the theory that if a traumatic situation happened to you in your past (infancy, childhood, teenage or young adult years) that the process to heal this issue must have a direct correlation to how long it will take you to heal the problem?

Resolving your health problems can happen quickly when you know how to get to your answer in 10 minutes or less. The place to begin is at the core of the emotional issues.

Your answers are in your body—every experience, event and situation. Everything that you have said or has been said to you is recorded in your body. These recordings are called cellular memory.

Your body memorizes all of your experiences from the moment you are conceived in your mother's womb. Your father's and your mother's ideas, their belief systems and their emotional states also affect you from the minute the sperm connects to the egg.

Your brain, much like a computer, cannot process all of this information. Your brain does not have the capacity to hold onto all of your personal data and information. So, your body stores the cellular memory of the information until you are ready to access it and heal yourself.

Children are not equipped to understand the ramifications of verbal and physical abuse or how the rest of their lives and relationships will be affected by it.

Your body records the experiences and your brain tries diligently to figure it all out. Your body and your brain eventually can't handle it, and you become ill and diagnosed with a specific "dis-ease."

The illness or mental challenges can last for years: talking about it, processing it, and re-verbalizing the same stories over and over again. The more you talk about it from your computer-brain, your body relives the experiences and re-traumatizes you over and over again. You can get caught up in these cycles of re-experiencing the traumas.

With the resolutions and solutions presented here, you can get to the core in 10 minutes or less and begin the "resolution progressive process." It involves your acceptance of the circumstances, understanding that your past cannot be changed and allowing you to believe that you can achieve a resolution for yourself, no matter what.

Where do you begin?

You must be willing to let go of belief systems which tell you that your answers are outside of you instead of inside of you.

You must be willing to let go of the belief that healing your emotional and physical issues takes a long time.

You must *stick to the relevant facts*. When you continue to tell your emotional stories over and over again, your computer-brain can't process your issues, and your physical body becomes stressed and strained.

Begin first with your willingness to look at yourself, your life and your emotional and physical issues from a *non-emotional vantage point*.

Begin with this intention. Say it out loud to all the cells in your body: *"I agree in this moment of my life to make the commitment to heal myself—no matter what!"*

1. I choose to be the non-emotional observer instead of an emotional victim of the unchangeable past.
2. I take full responsibility for myself without judging myself.
3. I take full charge of my life, and I let go of the circumstances and events of the unchangeable past which have controlled me, held me hostage and made me sick.
4. I take the progressive steps I require to move forward, regardless of what other people in my life may think or say about me.

5. I accept that I now create my life with conscious clarity.
6. I *believe* in myself, no matter what!

There is an emotional and physical answer for every diagnosis. You don't have to suffer. By the way, swelling in any area of your body is the watery physical emotion welling up in your body. An example of swelling is inflammation. Inflammation is the emotional and physical anger or rage being suppressed. Anger, resentment, frustration and fury are the tip of the inflammation iceberg.

Your body has the answers.

You must know how to ask yourself the correct questions. Do *not* ask your body, "What is wrong with you?" There is nothing wrong with you. It's how you have been emotionally and physically affected by a situation, condition or trauma in your past experiences. Or, it can be a re-triggering in your current situation which sets off an emotional reaction in you.

Getting to the core of an issue or problem means looking from a vantage point that does not have the emotional charge in the question. When you are emotionally charged, you cannot get to the facts of the situation. It's the emotional hooks to the past that make us sick in the first place.

Addressing the outside conditions, such as chemicals, toxins, drugs or alcohol accompanied by the emotional issues of heartbreak, abandonment, victimization and abuse, make the perfect contributing components which result in you being sick! You become weakened. Your body doesn't have the resistance. Wherever your body is weakest in your

DNA template, biology and limited, conditioned beliefs, you become sick.

The significance of illness is that the outside influences impacted and infected you right to your core. As a child, you could not possibly have the experience or understanding why these experiences were happening to you. When you were subjected to abuse and programmed to be a victim, it is inconceivable that the people around you (who are supposed to love, protect and guide you) might hurt you. *You carry that confusion and shock in your body for life until you have a resolution.*

Your body is an amazing resource for all of your experiences. With conscious clarity, begin to connect to your body. Begin asking yourself, "*Why* do I have this problem? *When* did it start?"

Here's a clue. Your illness began at the *origination point of the traumatic experience* which you could not believe or comprehend that this was happening to you.

Pain is your body's attempt to get your attention.

With fibromyalgia, the pain moves all over the body. Perhaps it is your entire body that is screaming for your attention. Drugs cover up the pain, while the emotional and physical issues in your physically and emotionally-challenged body make you sicker!

When children are abused and cannot process what is occurring, they "go out of the body." As an adult, you do the same thing. When things get rough, you disconnect and go to that place you created as a child to feel safe and hide. When this is happening, your body literally has to fend for itself! Illness and disease happen for reasons which are not always reasonable.

The other caveat of illness is that, as a child, you get the most attention from your parents or adults when you are sick. This establishes an unconscious dysfunctional pattern which says, "Well, if I get sick, someone will pay attention to me!" The country is full of people looking for attention, unconsciously using illness to get the attention that they are wanting or needing. Yet, it doesn't happen. It is difficult to be nurtured by yourself or anyone else when you are too sick or full of drugs to notice.

It's time to liberate your life! Now, to the point of getting your answer in 10 minutes or less.

Here are some life-changing steps which begin your progressive process. Read them out loud, and consider placing them in a place where you will see them often.

1. I am willing to get out of the story of my illness.
2. I recognize that I am not the illness or diagnosis.
3. I am willing to let go of the past, no matter how terrible it was.
4. I am willing to step into my power.
5. I am willing to detach emotionally from the past completely.
6. I am willing to accept full responsibility for myself without judgment.
7. I am willing to go inside myself for answers.
8. I am willing to accept the answers that I find.
9. I am willing to heal myself no matter what.
10. I am willing to accept myself completely!

Let your answers begin!

Go directly to the area of your body that is in crisis. Ask yourself, "What does it look like? Is it dark, heavy or thick?" You will know the description immediately! Create a room or a space for it with open doors and windows. You cannot be trapped in it. It is only a description to get you started.

In this space, ask yourself, "How old am I?" An age will arrive as an answer. Now, ask yourself, "What is going on at this age?" As the non-emotional observer, you will see the person or persons involved. You will "see" their fear and their emotional sickness which resulted from their fear. In this moment, it is time to stop being a victim of the past. Cut all emotional and physical attachments to the past.

Now, ask yourself, "What does the space look like now? Is it lighter or clearer?" As you clear the space, the area of your body with which you connected begins to heal at your cellular level. You are supporting your body to heal and get well.

Go to every area of your body and connect. Follow this same progressive process. Your body will give you your age and also the individuals who are involved as you glean the facts without the emotional attachments. You will comprehend that living in the past, regardless of the current time, is no longer relevant to you now. What happened— happened! You can't change the past!

What happens now is up to you. You are worthy of healing. Your body has all the answers. You need to ask the questions clearly, not to relive the trauma, but to get to the facts. A fact may be that someone abused you. The fact is they did. The fact is that time has passed. The fact is that this profile of someone abusing you in any way—verbally, physically or emotionally—is now no longer a profile in your life.

You choose how, when, where and why you participate in your life. You now choose with whom you participate. You are now in relationships with people with whom you can relate. This is the power of being the conscious creator of your life!

Create powerfully, and you will never succumb to being powerless again! Say this as many times as you feel you require. Say it as you connect to all of the places in your body which you require to heal.

Knowing at my deepest knowing, I cannot change the past, but what I can do is release the past from my cellular memory where it no longer serves me.

Forgiveness means giving myself the opportunity, as the observer only, to go back to that origination point of my experience and be willing to see that the person (father, mother, teacher, sibling, abuser) is more afraid than me.

He, she or they had no idea who I am or who I was at that time. All he, she or they had were fears and limited belief systems which impacted them to act this way.

What happened is not acceptable, but I can no longer hold the experience or experiences in my body. The time has come to free myself from the unchangeable past and release all of the physical and emotional attachments.

This is the statement of freedom!

I cannot change the past, it was one minute ago.
But I can change my future; it is one minute from now.
By not dragging the past forward where it no longer serves
me, I am freeing myself.

Getting your answer in 10 minutes or less is the beginning and not the end. It is the starting point for resolution. As you resolve the emotional and physical attachments to the relationships, issues and illnesses which resulted from the physical and emotional traumas, you are on a new path where you walk fully in charge of your life!

You make clear choices which influence and affect your life consciously. No longer are decisions made for you by someone else's agendas or opinions which are controlling your life.

You have begun the progressive process through your connection to the infinite intelligence and intellect of your body which is where your answers live. Now, you can make empowered choices for your journey. You are actively involved in your healing.

The resolution means it is resolved in your cellular memory. You now begin to create your solutions. The solution means that you are solving and dissolving your issues and emotional and physical traumas at the core, which is at your cellular level of consciousness within you.

Now with the resolution, *you* are the solution!

Through the Anshara Method of Accelerated Healing and Abundance, you are guided to connect to your unlimited intelligence and intellect to utilize your intuition and to access your clear, cellular memory. You empower yourself to be the conscious, deliberate, focused and energized creator of your life! Enjoy becoming the best power-full and power-filled you!

CHAPTER

Twenty-Two

Love Your Whole Self, Love Yourself Whole
by Dr. Vicki L. High

DR. VICKI L. HIGH

Dr. Vicki L. High is a best-selling author, founder of Heart 2 Heart Healing, life coach, counselor, speaker, and former mayor. Dr. High, a pioneer in spiritual healing, boldly journeys into new frontiers of healing, love, empowerment and spiritual insights. She shares wisdom through direct experience in healing, intuition, and spiritual realms. Her gifts empower her to connect ideas and concepts and create patterns for life and healing. She lives through her heart, honoring each person as an aspect of God–Source.

Vhigh4444@aol.com www.heart2heartconnections.us
www.empowereddreams.com @heart2heartprograms
@stoptraumadrama, @kalmingkids, @empowereddreams

Acknowledgments

Diane Sellers, Darlene Owen, Jamie Norman, Janene Cates Putnam, Mayza Clark, and Stacey McGown

Love Your Whole Self,
Love Yourself Whole
By Dr. Vicki L. High

Betrayal. Adultery. Divorced in 73 days. My heart shattered like a stained-glass window along with my dreams. My life, as I knew it, was gone. Everything changed: my husband, my family, my work. I felt unloved, broken and unlovable. I never suspected that, through this pain, I would discover an incredible pathway to love my whole self and love myself whole! It was not an overnight journey.

A coworker dragged this Baptist girl to a Reiki session. When the Reiki Master placed her hand on my heart and said, "You have a broken heart, but it's starting to heal," she captured my undivided attention. Then she blew me away. I heard the truth in her voice when she said, "A long time ago in a far-away place, you gave me something that I needed, and now it's my turn to give back to you." Within two months, I was training to become a Reiki Master Teacher. It was a gateway and, like a phoenix, my heart began to heal as I rose from the ashes of my former life. A whole new world unfolded before me. My journey to love my whole self had begun.

My Reiki Master asked me to prepare some publicity opportunities for a healer she had invited to our community. I naïvely called the ABC Studio and scheduled him to be on the morning news program. When he arrived, a voice outside my ear said clearly, "You will work for this man." I promptly dismissed this wisdom from its disembodied voice. I owned and operated two companies, served as President of the Economic Development Corporation, Mayor Pro-Tem, and Chamber of Commerce Publicity Director. I was a busy "human doing" rather than a human being.

My Baptist roots warred with my heart's yearning for knowledge. In two days, I attended the healing seminar with a friend. My friend said she didn't understand the process, so I offered for her to try the healing technique on me. Amidst the anxiety and worry about stepping out beyond my faith, I immediately felt a large, warm hand clasp my hand and wrist. As a domestic violence survivor, I was alarmed that some stranger was touching me. I could see, but my eyes were closed. I saw Jesus standing there in his robe and sandals. When I looked into His eyes, I recognized Him. He knew me, and I knew Him. It felt like a benediction. I was exactly where I needed to be.

Jesus looked deeply into my eyes and said, "Vicki, you are loved. You are special. You are in my care." All I could do was cry. My life changed in that moment. Later, I realized Jesus activated my sacred heart. Other healing modalities focus on the scientific perspective, but I knew that the sacred heart was the true source of power and healing.

I experienced miracles. People spoke on my table, but at first, I thought it was the person on the table. Then I heard, "We're from the stars." Suddenly everything changed. Later I was told, "You allowed us to connect." I began to hear the most amazing words from these masters, angels, and guides. I was a sponge and wanted to soak up every word they shared. Once they told me, "Before you were born, God kissed your eyes, kissed your lips and anointed your soul." On another occasion they said, "The [sacred] heart cannot lie to you." I had never heard these words, and I felt God and the Masters were teaching me directly. It was exciting to hear and experience the intimacy of God's love for each of us. I changed from the inside out.

Healing experiences continued. Miracles happened during sessions. I just knew that my sacred heart was the power center and, when activated, Unconditional Love flowed through my sacred heart to change lives. In one message, Jesus said, "When I heal people, I heal them heart to heart. I speak to people from heart to heart." That's when my gift, Heart 2 Heart, was named. Heart 2 Heart taught me to tap into this amazing gift within each of us. Heart 2 Heart is powered by Unconditional Love—God.

When I work through the sacred heart, I feel I access the throne room of God through my very own "Holy of Holies." Each of us has this sacred place within us. It's the most amazing ride of my life. Since 2002, hundreds and perhaps thousands of people have been transformed by the power of Unconditional Love, Heart 2 Heart Healing. Here are a few examples.

When I shared a healing session with a chiropractor, I felt compelled to work on his hand. Later, he explained he had injured it in a car wreck and spent thousands of dollars to restore the full use of his hand. However, all attempts had failed. He exclaimed, "I can see tissue forming on my fingers. There's a blue light coming out of your hand!" The next day, he excitedly called to report his hand had healed. It was amazing!

One healing client provided a detailed description of angels in the room. This client also described a gift of "siloquia," that allowed us to interact with, see, and hear messages from angels and the heavens. During this same experience, St. Francis of Assisi announced his presence, but stipulated, "I'm not a sissy. I'm Assisi." You had to love his sense of humor!

My cousin, an avid hunter and paralyzed veteran, has been in a wheelchair for almost 40 years. After his hunting trips, his legs swell, and he stays in bed for two days to let the fluid drain. One day, I offered a Heart 2 Heart healing session. I began the process. After about 10 minutes, I asked him what his legs looked like after two days. He replied, "They look like dishpan hands, only legs." I looked down and said, "I think it's done." He said, "No way!" He threw the covers back and the fluid had drained out of his legs. Recently, he was admitted to the hospital. The doctors told his wife that he was dying and would not last through the night. What I know for sure is that only Source knows the exact moment of our death. I told her to advocate for him and Heart 2 Heart practitioners began distance healing on him. I visited him, in person, weeks later. The doctors couldn't explain what happened. (Caution: miracle in progress!) He was thriving. He still had a few obstacles, but he was looking forward to going home again.

A marvelous woman was suffering from gall bladder cancer and had developed sepsis in her throat. She was advised to say her final goodbyes, but I couldn't be there in person because I was teaching a workshop. During the lesson on distance healing, I provided only her first name to the student assigned to work on her and no other information. He began the healing process, and then he reported, "She has the sweetest energy. I worked on her torso and her throat." He had no idea what her illness was, but he worked on those exact locations. The doctors couldn't explain it. They said she had been blessed with a miracle and sent her home from the hospital two days later.

I have witnessed miracles of babies born to mothers who lost hope of having children. I have worked on children who became healed in the womb. Doctors suggest terminating these pregnancies because of expected birth defects they diagnosed before delivery. I am more convinced than ever that this healing is a gift from God who creates us. Doctors prepare expecting parents for the worst outcomes that aren't likely to happen. God is the ultimate authority and knows far more than we humans can possibly know. God, with the help of healers, provides healing or re-creates bodies in ways that doctors can't even imagine or explain. These are parents who have been traumatized with fear that their baby would be born with defects, and because of their faith, they could not terminate the pregnancy. Imagine their joy when their baby is born whole and healthy!

One Heart 2 Heart practitioner was kicked by a horse in the arm and neck, while another practitioner immediately began Heart 2 Heart Healing in the ambulance on the way to the hospital. Doctors placed a pin in her injured elbow and a cast on her arm. More practitioners began to provide Heart 2 Heart Healing. Four weeks later, the x-ray showed no break at all in her arm—not a repaired bone. It looked as if the bone had never been broken, even though the pin was still in her elbow.

Heart 2 Heart helps people suffering through chemo and radiation treatments. It has been a factor in cases where tumors have disappeared. According to the Masters, Heart 2 Heart heals DNA. A coworker's husband had stomach cancer. We arranged to go to her home during lunch to provide Heart 2 Heart Healing. After a single treatment, the doctor reported there was no more stomach cancer. I love this work!

Some special experiences linger in your memory. A man diagnosed with a brain tumor and oat cell cancer came to a Heart 2 Heart Healing demonstration. He was weak from both the disease and treatments he was receiving. He lay on the table for only 3-4 minutes before it became too painful for him to lie there. During that time, another participant reported, "I saw a tiny angel at his head." His wife reported she smelled roses so strong that she could taste them. Three days later, they came to find me and shared he had been sleeping a lot. Although it alarmed the doctors, a healing sleep is a normal occurrence in Heart 2 Heart Healing. After his checkup, they reported, "The doctor danced down the hall with the CAT scan in his hands as he said, 'You can frame this. The brain tumor is gone.'"

In one case, a friend asked casually what I did. I agreed to demonstrate as she lay on the massage table. I began the session and moved over her abdomen. I stopped because of what I call "energy feedback," and hovered over that area knowing the Heart 2 Heart Healing was flowing. She asked me what I found. I kept working on her but suggested she go to the gynecologist for a checkup. She responded that she had already scheduled an appointment. When I called to follow up, she told me that her doctor said her tissue looked precancerous. The doctor took a biopsy and sent it to the lab. The lab technician called to verify what it was they were testing because the tissue looked healthy when it arrived. The tissue in her body was already in the process of being healed, but the biopsied tissue, the same non-local DNA, was being healed at the same time even though she and her biopsied tissue were physically in two different locations. That's quantum physics!

Heart 2 Heart Healing doesn't only work on people. It also works on animals, plants and situations. I was asked to work on a friend's horse, diagnosed with cancer. She was harnessed in the barn as I stood heart to heart with her. As the energy began to flow, the barn dog plastered himself against the backs of my legs and the mare reached around me with her neck to pull me closer into her heart. It was awesome! On another occasion, I was working on horses in the barn when they began stomping their hooves demanding sessions, too.

I continued to see outcomes of healing sessions that mesmerized the scientist in me. Since the beginning, I journaled, tracked trends, asked questions and collected data. My goal, at some point, will be to collate the data and provide solid evidence of healings reported since 2002.

Heart 2 Heart Healing has generated other programs which transform lives. When used in Empowered Dreams, people architect lives they truly want to live. When used in Mini-Me and Draining Relationship Exercises, people dump junk from their trunk, healing and resolving issues. These exercises transform traumas and obstacles into stepping stones for an empowered future. When used in Kalming Kids, it triggers a catalyst for change that empowers teachers to transform energy in classrooms into more loving, supportive environments. When used in Recovering Humanity programs, people create lives beyond hopelessness, incarceration and addictions. When used in Stop Trauma Drama, people suffering from PTSD, abuse and violence change their coping habits and heal trauma. The transformational power of Heart 2 Heart Healing changes lives and makes a positive difference in our world.

I know these programs work because they changed my life and the lives of many others. There have been personal benefits, too. A coworker asked me to make some changes to documents and databases. As I sat down at the computer, I quickly moved through the to-do list. She reached over and touched my arm, and as I looked at her, she asked, "What did you just do?" Puzzled, I asked her, "What are you talking about?" She replied, "You moved so fast through each step. How could you read so fast?" She made me aware that I read the entire page of information at a glance, made the change and moved on to the next item. My spiritual gifts have expanded. I am still a human with faults and warts, but I have grown to realize Unconditional Love, God, is the most powerful change agent in the Universe. The Masters advised, "No rules. No restrictions. No limitations. No boundaries."

When I thought about those dark days in my life, I remembered I read this book, The Celestine Prophecy, by James Redfield. It was an "A-ha!" moment for me when I realized that I lit the fuse that ignited my world. Those insights Redfield shared were catalysts that exploded and destroyed my old life, placing me in the crucible to burn off the junk so that I could love my whole self and love myself whole. Unconditional Love opened an amazing landscape, the most beautiful place I had ever seen. It brought me healing and wholeness beyond my imagination. The greatest blessing was the wealth of love, deep understanding and conversations with God, Jesus, and the Masters that opened my heart.

Anytime I provide a healing session, I receive one. I heal others. I heal myself. I love myself. I love others. I learned to look for the blessing in healing and loving myself. It's there among the rubble of my life and yours. It can lead to happiness if we are courageous enough to let go of the old and make room for something awesomely beyond our imaginations! Let's cast fear aside. Let's love our whole selves and love ourselves whole!

Heart 2 Heart Healing Frequency Awakening:

1. Visualize a ball of fiber optic yarn in your hands as you hold it at your heart. This ball will initially be around the size of a grapefruit. You've always had this energy within you, but you may not have been aware of it.

2. Based on your spiritual gifts, you may sense the energy. You may see the energy, hear a tone or experience an energetic vibration. It may even manifest as cool or warm air. If you cannot see, hear or sense the energy ball, slowly rotate your hands until you experience a sensation of the energy.

3. Expand the ball of light by pulling the energy like taffy. Make a note of any changes in the energy itself. If you can't feel it, then bring your hands closer together until you

are aware of the ball of light. Then begin to stretch the ball of light again.

4. To share this awakening experience, stretch your ball of light wide enough to allow another person to place her hand within your ball of light. Move your ball of light around her hand. Ask her to describe her personal experience. The energy is moving through her hand even if, at first, she cannot feel it. If you feel the energy ball, the energy is moving through you to the other person, and then back to you.

This energy is powered by the galactic frequency of Unconditional Love that exists outside of time and space. It is transformational energy. Trust its ability to access the body where emotional, physical, mental or spiritual issues exist. Use this energy to reduce stress. Experiment with it frequently as you observe what happens. Allow it to teach and heal you from the inside, out.

Final Thoughts From The Publisher

It has been a true honor to work with the healers in this and all our other incredible books. If you would like to join us on your authorship journey we would love to have you

Visit us at

www.asyouwishpublishing.com

We are always looking for new and seasoned authors to be a part of our collaborative books.

If you would like to write your own book please reach out to Kyra Schaefer at kyra@asyouwishpublishing.

Recently Released

Happy Thoughts Playbook

When I Rise, I Thrive

Flame and Sparkles: The Magic Within by Isaac Bowers

Healer: 22 Expert Healers Share Their Wisdom To Help You Transform

Upcoming Projects

Life Coach: 22 Expert Coaches Help You Reclaim Your Passion, Purpose and Personal Power

Inspirations: 100 Personal Uplifting Stories For Daily Happiness

The Nudge by Felicia Shaviri

Made in the USA
Middletown, DE
27 March 2019